LOVERS, DREAMERS, & THIEVES

My people, Chicago, & the Polish bakery where I grew up

MARCIA CEBULSKA

Flint Hills Publishing

LOVERS, DREAMERS, & THIEVES
My people, Chicago, & the Polish bakery where I grew up

Cover Design by Amy Albright

stonypointgraphics.weebly.com

Flint Hills Publishing
Topeka, Kansas
Tucson, Arizona
www.flinthillspublishing.com

Printed in the U.S.A.

This book reflects the author's present recollections
of experiences over time and from her perspective.
Some events and dialogue have been recreated.

Paperback Book: ISBN: 978-1-953583-48-2
Hardback Book ISBN: 978-1-953583-47-5
Electronic Book ISBN: 978-1-953583-49-9

These essays originally appeared in the following publications:
"Hazel, or My First Public Reading Was in a Supermarket"
in the author's book, *Skywriting;*
"The Oat Field" and "Nun Dolls" in *Inscape;*
"Women in Veils" in the blog of Lisa A. Kramer.

Library of Congress Control Number: 2023904452

For my storyteller grandmother,

Victoria Migała Kozial,

gone but still alive.

MY PEOPLE
(Some of them, anyway.)

BACK ROW L to R: Walter "Mike" Mika (Helene's husband & my
uncle); Joseph Kozial (my mother's brother & my uncle); Dolores Kozial
(my mother's sister & my aunt); Walter "Wally" Kozial (my mother's
brother & my godfather); Walter "Wally" Cebulski (my father)

MIDDLE ROW L to R: Helene Kozial Mika (my mother's sister &
my auntie); Victoria M. Kozial (my mother's mother & my
grandmother); Stanley "Stashu" Kozial (my mother's brother & my
uncle); Stanley (my mother's father & my grandfather);
Casmira "Casey" Cebulski (my mother)

FRONT ROW L to R: Walter "Porky" Mika (Helene & Mike's son
& my cousin); Richard Cebulski (Casey & Wally's son & my brother)

CONTENTS

Introduction *11*

The So-Called "Weaker Sex"
The Blacksmith *17*
Animal House *21*
Women in Veils *23*
Hazel, or My First Public Reading
Was in a Supermarket *27*
East of the Sun & West of the Moon 29
Crowded *33*

In the Limelight
The Ring *39*
Upstairs/Downstairs at St. Stan's *43*
Miss Gloria *49*
My Gay Fiancé *55*
The Race *61*

The American Dream
The Story of My Grandparents' Rise and Fall,
1917–1930, Told in Pictures *67*

Home and Away
The Vase *75*
Pink Neon *79*
Polish Easter *85*
Hot Chili *91*

Rebels with a Cause
Snuggies *95*
Quick to Speak *101*
The Last President of Everything *105*
Little Fart *109*
Shakespeare's Not for You *111*
Gefilte Fish *113*

Escape and Other Entertainments
Mom, Dad, Auntie Helene, & Uncle Mike Having
Fun Long Before I Was Born *115*
Florida *117*
Smok *119*
The Oat Field *125*
The Devil and the Tailor *127*
The Polka King *129*

The Family that Prays Together, Stays Together
Nun Dolls *137*
Sunstroke *141*
The Gambler *145*
The Crush *153*

Fame and Shame
Sha Sha and Chi Chi *159*
A Made Man *163*
The R.W. Simms Building *165*
Rejection *169*
Fame and Shame *171*
My Own Personal Donald *175*

Saying Goodbye
Revisiting the Old Neighborhood *175*
Visiting Busia *183*
On the Skids *185*
The Sins of the Father *189*
A Eulogy for Mom *193*
Farewell to Richard *195*
Sooooooo Big!!!!! *197*

Appendix: Excerpts from Creative Work *199*

Acknowledgments *211*

About the Author *213*

INTRODUCTION

I was a miniature nun in kindergarten. The Feds took my father away in handcuffs. My mother was in love with a priest. The memories came flooding in as I pulled individual photos out of the big blue storage containers my mother and grandmother had left me decades earlier. A grandfather with his peddler's wagon. My mother dressed as a harem girl at a costume party. I emptied the bins onto the dining room table.

Like most writers, I have drawn on my life, my family, and my friends for the stories and characters in my work. I believe my best writing has come from life lived and remembered, especially episodes that left me delighted, scared, regretful, or curious. My father's gambling. My grandmother kicking her shoe across the room when she told her own Polish version of "Cinderella." This memoir is about the saints and sinners who shaped my writing and my life.

Turns out you can't always rely on hearsay and memory. I learned that my grandmother lied about her age on the immigrant boat from Hamburg. My father's case involved the Secret Service and a lie detector expert. Some stories had been reduced in the telling because of shame. Others embellished for the sake of glory. I sometimes felt the need to add details to help depict a character I knew well or to paint a picture of a place or time. What kind of toys did we have in 1950? Why did my grandmother buy that vase? My friend Cecil talks about the need, when storytelling, to "tart it up a bit." Good storytelling sometimes requires tarting it up a bit to paint a clearer picture, convey a complex character. Just as fiction can sometimes get at truth better than a statistic, storytelling can sometimes get at truth through the creative use of illustrative details. Guilty as charged.

One day I sat down at my computer and typed the sentence, "My cousin Susan married a pig farmer." And so, it began. "My cousin Wally collects nun dolls." "My great-grandmother was a blacksmith." Every day for months I poured out a story that began with "My." Each of them seemed to be waiting for me when I put my fingers to the keys. Every day a story that made me laugh or cry or shiver.

And now, I give them to you.

"what shoots above are roots"

– Michael Kleber-Diggs in *Worldly Things*

The So-Called

"Weaker Sex"

My great-grandparents with 8 of their 12 children.

THE BLACKSMITH

My great-grandmother was a blacksmith. That's right, a blacksmith. And we're not just talking horseshoes here. My mother's mother's mother hammered gates, chains, and sickles out of red-hot metal. She forged tools for the villagers and carriage wheels for the lord of the manor, the *pan*.

Me? Some people call me a wordsmith. I metaphorically hammer sentences and paragraphs out of the inky shapes on the page. Typing on my computer keyboard, I move prepositions and semicolons around in the hopes that I can end up with a play or a story somebody might want to read.

My foremother went on to birth 12 children. It was the 19th century in what is now Poland, then under Austrian rule. She and her family lived in a two-room house under a feudal economy in which it was a crime to take a fish from a stream or a wild berry from a bush. The *pan* had the absolute right of life or death over his subjects.

In my spacious Victorian home, I complain that the air conditioning doesn't do a very good job of cooling my writing room. I gave birth to one single child. I eat raspberries and yogurt from the supermarket for breakfast and I have the right to vote.

My mother's mother's mother learned to forge wagon wheels and axe blades from her father, who was paid by the *pan* largely in vodka, a drink that made him less and less able to ply his trade. She learned well and went on to teach smithery to the man who would become my great-grandfather. Passing through her village on his way to Hamburg, where he planned to board a ship to America, he'd been looking for a few days' work. He had a substantial moustache, played the concertina, and sang. He stayed a lifetime. Together, my great-grandparents labored and sang their hearts out. Worked long hours and danced with their children. They never made it to America, but their daughter Wiktoria (Victoria in English), my future grandmother, shipped off from Hamburg and headed to the U.S.A. to become a guest worker when she was fifteen.

When I was about to leave for a leisure trip to Europe, my grandmother told me the story of her blacksmith mother. It made me want to visit my grandmother's town of Dębica. I traveled during the time of Soviet Russian domination. Long lines of hopeful customers stood for hours in front of butcher shops, where only one or two links of sausage hung from hooks. In the few dress stores that were open, exactly one style was displayed: long, black, plain. It was a time of privation, but as I strolled the dusty paths, I reminded myself that I was walking in my foremothers' footsteps.

My grandmother's brother Franciszek and his family opened their home to me. A stove decorated with hand-painted tiles heated the house and produced huge quantities of edibles. Despite the environment of deprivation and hunger, my great-aunts and cousins hosted me with baked hams and filled dumplings, meaty stews, and cheeses. It was clear that they had to beg, borrow, and steal to obtain the provisions. They had traded beloved objects on the black market to cover the table with food and drink. I was the first and only one of my great-grandmother's American-born descendants to visit.

When I sat down at the groaning table, the women of the family stood behind the chairs, ready to refill the plates. If one spoonful of dilled potatoes was eaten, two more spoonfuls replaced it. I had to leave my plate overflowing for my hosts to know that I was satisfied. No Clean Plates Club at that table. A smiling great-uncle played the fiddle. Another, the concertina. Everyone sang and laughed. The room was filled with joy and borrowed abundance.

Having grown up in an immigrant neighborhood, I knew a smattering of Polish. In a garbled version of my great-grandmother's tongue, I asked about her. My relatives were delighted to tell me about her smithy. It was still in the family. They were so glad I asked. The great-uncle who had played the fiddle pointed to himself with a smile. He, yes, he still plied the trade. He led a procession of family members to his home about a mile away, where custom demanded that we sit down to dine once again. When I was seated at the table, he showed me a large, framed photograph of my great-grandparents surrounded by eight of their children. It was the first time I'd seen their likenesses.

After the second dinner, I followed my blacksmith great-uncle down a well-worn path behind the house to an old stone building. He unlatched and swung open the double doors. Sunlight illuminated a cave-like room with ancient uneven walls. I faced a carved stone table that stood at the height of an altar, its surfaces rounded off by time like stones in a stream. Above it was a large opening, like that of the bread oven in my parents' bakery, covered with a patina of centuries-old soot, shiny as a new black shoe. I tried to picture my great-grandmother wielding a hot hammer, sweating over the anvil, but I failed. In the photograph I had just seen of her, she was a small, slender, gentle-looking woman dressed in her Sunday best. Nevertheless, I had to wipe tears off my cheek. I could feel her in my bones.

ANIMAL HOUSE

My mother always kept a dog and a bird. She was the kind of pet-mother who would tell you that her dachshund Wiggles preferred his chicken roasted rather than boiled. In the bakery days, she had a dog named Cinders, who we affectionately called Cindy. She was from the same litter as my Auntie Helene's dog Eclipse, born during, yes, an eclipse. They were both black with a little white trim on the face and tail. Eclipse was a cuddle bunch but not terribly well trained. Cinders, on the other hand, knew how to sit up, jump on command, roll over, and stay. My mother's bird, Skippy, often rode on the top of Cindy's head.

My mother's dogs never had leashes or walks around the block. My mom just opened the kitchen door and Cindy would step out to do her business, then bark a couple of times to be let back in. Occasionally, Skippy the bird would get a ride out into the world on Cindy's head from which he would fly straight up into the sky. When my mother noticed Skippy's absence, she would walk outside, clap her hands, and immediately Skippy would come sailing down to land on her shoulder. My mother's pets never wanted to leave her, so they hurried back to her tethered by homemade treats and love.

When my brother and I washed dishes, Skippy sometimes divebombed into the dishwater. We'd scream, "Mom, Mom!" and she'd come running, pulling a wet, soapy Skippy out of the water, then lovingly rinse out Skippy's beak with clear water and wrap him in a towel, gently drying the bird that looked up at her adoringly. Skippy knew how to say "Gimme kiss," and usually followed the phrase with a loud smacking sound. He rewarded Mom with many kisses every time she saved him.

My mom used to hold business meetings with the visiting salesmen from the bakery supply companies in our kitchen, her office. She sometimes plied them with shots of scotch at our kitchen table, bargaining for a good deal on flour or cherry preserves. But she drew a strict line and booted them out when any of them got flirty. A closed door separated the kitchen/office from the private rooms such as the living room and bedrooms. One time, my mother was behind the folding screen which separated our living room from my parent's bedroom, changing from her work clothes to a nice suit. She was down to her skivvies when she heard a loud wolf whistle and quickly covered herself up. She called out, "Go away!" and looked around, ready to give hell to whichever salesman was eyeing her. But it was Skippy, sitting atop the screen, practicing the latest addition to his vocabulary.

WOMEN IN VEILS

My brief life as a woman in a veil started when this photo was taken. When a friend invited me to write a guest blog, I wrote this essay to accompany the photo.

I've been thinking about changing my Facebook photo to one of me dressed as a nun. Yeah, this one, where I'm smiling with baby teeth but ensconced in the starchy white and woolly brown habit of the Franciscan Sisters of the Blessed Kunegunda. That's right,

Kunegunda. Tom, my husband, laughs when he sees the picture. Most people do, maybe because of the incongruity of a kindergartner wearing a wimple, or maybe they're remembering *Nunsense*. The Sisters I recall from my 13 years of Catholic schooling were neither ridiculous nor mean. None of them rapped my fingers with a ruler. And yes, Sister Liam was comical while teaching physics, but her antics forever instilled in me the upside of making a point with humor. As an adult, I've given up going to church, but I still admire the women who inspired the guiding principles for my life and work: the necessity for social action, the importance of knowledge, and the value of community among women.

So how did I get into this picture anyway, wearing a veil more complicated than a burka? It was the centennial celebration of Chicago's Holy Name Cathedral parish. Two little kids were chosen to represent each neighborhood church in the city and dressed in miniature duplication of its nuns and priests. I was thrilled to be chosen. Home movies show a grand procession of us befrocked children snaking around downtown and eventually into the glorious Holy Name Cathedral, where bishops and archbishops resplendent in red and gold regalia enthralled us with pomp and ceremony.

In contrast, our own parish nuns were, like the current Pope Francis, devoted to simplicity, social action, humility, and poverty. They were committed to the people of our neighborhood where the factory smokestacks loomed just a block away from the church steeple and where most of the women wore housedresses and babushkas. Sometimes I see photographs of women from Saudi Arabia wearing scarves tied just like theirs. We all had to cover our heads in church so we didn't tempt men with our glorious hair. My own mother, a woman of style, wore couture and hats, often with a wisp of black veiling over her eyes.

Mom had tried being a nun. She had entered the convent as a postulant when she was 15 but didn't last a year. She returned to high school and took an after-school job working at a bakery, where she met a young man who she'd marry when she turned 18. Ever after, she flaunted her unnunness whenever possible, wearing filmy harem pants to costume parties and dancing the can-can for a fundraiser. But she always had close friends who were in the convent. She brought them treats and had them over for martinis. When her nun friends came to our house, they'd try on her clothes, page through *Glamour* magazine, and laugh with her, conspiratorially and often. Then, having had their brief holiday, they dressed again in their formal habits to do their self-effacing good work. And my mom would go on to deliver bread and pastries from our bakery to the poor, old, and sick members of the parish.

By the time I was in high school, we lived in the suburbs and the Dominican Sisters who taught me stood proud with straight backs. They wore soft white robes and black veils. It was rumored that every nun at our high school had a doctorate, having been drafted from a college to open the new school for girls. Every classroom had a copy of Thomas Aquinas's *Summa Theologica*. If we asked a pesky question, we were told to go "to the *Summa*" to seek an answer. I learned to do research, decline Latin verbs, discuss world literature, converse in French, and sing Gregorian chant. I played Dido in a shadow play adaptation of *The Aeneid*. I felt inspired and awakened. In off hours, the Sisters roller skated in the basement.

Nuns lived in community. When my mother took me to the convent for visits, I found it quiet, peaceful, and scented with holy water. The women chatted in subdued tones in the dim sitting room. Mom would squeeze a dollar bill into a hand or kiss a cheek before leaving. Sometimes she would drive Sister Dolorine to visit her family in Cleveland. They would speak in Polish so that I, sitting in the back seat, wouldn't understand the secrets they shared. They would laugh and cry together, forging a bond, celebrating their commonality. At home my mom raised a family and ran a business, balancing a difficult husband, bakers, salesmen, and ledgers. With her nun friends, she reached across to assure and be assured, offering support, a joke, or a hug. They shared lives so different yet so much the same, dealing with affronts, greed, pride, jealousy, humanness, womanness. They were part of the community of women. I watched, and I learned.

I am grateful to nuns. Those women who lived a seemingly medieval life inspired me to have the confidence to take risks in the name of justice and peace. They were the most educated women I knew, and they taught me not to allow my gender to hold me back in the pursuit of knowledge and self-actualization. Like my mom, they were far from perfect, sometimes impatient. But from them, I learned to respect and value friendship among women and, yes, the benefits of a well-earned break.

My grandfather, Sister Angeline, Mom, and
Sister Dolorine on my grandparents' farm.

HAZEL,
or MY FIRST PUBLIC READING WAS IN A SUPERMARKET

Me, in high school.

When I was 16, I worked as a checkout girl in a suburban Jewel Food Store. My boss was named Hazel. She had the face of a bulldog and a personality to match. We were all a bit frightened of her stern voice reprimanding us about how we had slacked off by chatting with the other checkers instead of serving customers. Or not tidying up the shelves of canned goods during unbusy minutes. Every day, at 5 p.m., Hazel pulled down the microphone that hung from the ceiling at the front of the store. Into this instrument, usually used to call for more checkers or bag boys, she said "Goodnight" to each department head, name by name. "Goodnight, Howard. Goodnight, Rudy. Goodnight, Sam." Like that. None of us quite understood how this fit in with her otherwise menacing personality.

One day in the break room, I scribbled a bit of verse entitled "Poem to be Read to the Sound of a Cash Register." Hazel asked to see what I was writing. She read and re-read. "C'mon," she said and led me down the stairs to the front of the store. Using the hanging mic, Hazel instructed everyone in the store—employees and customers alike—to stop and listen. She handed me the microphone and instructed me to start reading my poem when she gave me the signal. Hazel poised herself behind a counter, nodded her head, and provided background sounds on a register as I read aloud. "Chigetty-chug, Chigetty-chug, Chigetty-chigetty-chigetty-chug." Lines about cans of beans and produce greens followed. Rhymes about stock boys hauling and babies bawling.

A month later, a boy named Alan asked me if I had seen the company newsletter: "It's on the bulletin board in the break room." And there it was, with my poem circled and my name underlined. Hazel had sent it in to the national office, giving me encouragement for a possible career playing with words.

EAST OF THE SUN &
WEST OF THE MOON

My grandmother covered her face in embarrassment, but underneath her fingers we could see her smile. My Uncle Stash was prodding her to tell the story of when, in her home country of Poland, a sword fight had been fought over her. "Tell them about the swords, about that guy named Pigeon who was in love with you," Stash insisted.

"Go-womp," she answered. Or rather, that's how it sounded to my young ears. All I could think of was the Polish word for stuffed cabbage, a favorite dish. But what was this about my grandmother being the reason for a sword fight? "His name was Gołąb, like in *gołąbki*, you know, what you eat."

"The sword fight!"

"Yes, yes. They were boys, they pulled out their swords. Gołąb means pigeon, the stuffed cabbages look like pigeons when you serve them. Poorer people like us made the stuffed cabbage because that's what we had. Cabbages."

"They wore swords? A guy named Pigeon was in a swordfight over you?"

"It was long time ago, you know it was long time ago, there was a poor man who was very proud of his daughter." Busia, our beloved matriarch, began a story over the remains of a Thanksgiving dinner. Clearly, she was avoiding telling us about the sword fight, but we knew and loved the story she had started instead, so we let her go on. "The poor peasant man bragged so much that word even got to the king! And the king was so tired of hearing about this smart girl, he ordered the poor father to come to him and he told the man that he wanted to meet this smart girl. And, if the girl was as smart as he said, he, the king would marry her. If not, there would be serious consequences.

"The poor man bowed deeply and went home to his daughter. 'The king said you must come to the palace when it is morning but not morning, you must come riding but not riding, walking but not walking, dressed but not dressed. And you must give him a gift but not give him a gift.'

"The old man apologized for getting his daughter into this terrible situation.

"'Don't worry, Father, just bring me a goat and tie it outside the house. And bring me a dove in a cage. And your old pajamas, the ones with the holes that I keep telling you to throw away.'

"When he brought her the old pajamas, she tore them up even more so there were great big holes in the cloth. When it was almost the dawn, she came to the palace door and demanded to see the great king.

"The light was just starting to come in the sky, it was just about the dawn. Night but not night, day but not day. She was wearing the old holey pajamas. Dressed but not dressed. And straddling the goat with her feet on the ground. Riding but not riding, walking but not walking. She held a dove in her hand and when she reached toward him to give it to him, she let go and it flew away. She gave him a gift but didn't give him a gift.

"The king nodded his head. 'You are as smart as your father said and I will marry you tomorrow. But there is one condition. You must never meddle in my business. Never.' The girl nodded her head and asked that there be a room in the palace for her father since he was getting old. The king agreed and there was great feasting for three days.

"The years passed, and the couple lived happy together. But then, one night, there was a knock on the door. The people at the door needed to have some papers signed by midnight but the king was out of town. The queen waited until nearly midnight for the king to return but his train was late, and he didn't come. She asked if she could sign the papers in his stead and the men said yes, she could. And so she did.

"But when the king came home, he was angry and sent the queen to their summer palace to live, never to come back to the main palace again. She understood his decision but asked, 'Can I take one thing, just one thing from this palace that I like very much?' And the king, thinking it was maybe a picture or a vase, said yes.

"'And also,' asked the queen, 'can we have tea together, like we usually do, tonight, just one last time?' And again, the king said yes, he would like that too. The queen went to the servants and asked them to put a special sleeping powder in the king's tea. The two of them had their tea together and then the king fell asleep in their bed, so soundly he didn't notice when the servants carried the bed onto a wagon. And, in this way, he was carried to the summer palace.

"In the morning, the king woke up, saw his wife, and said, 'What are you doing here!? You are supposed to be in the summer palace!'

"And the queen answered, 'And I am here, in the summer palace. Look around!' And he did.

"He said, 'Then, what I am doing here?'

"She smiled and said, 'You said I could bring my favorite thing, and you are my favorite thing, so I brought you.'

"And the king and queen lived there in the *dvor*, the summer palace, for the rest of their living days."

So, we passed around the pumpkin pie. None of us felt like asking more about sword fighting.

CROWDED

My maternal grandmother as a young woman.

My grandmother quit school after the 4th grade because, as she put it, she "didn't like the crowds." I had loved school and the great numbers of children, so I was surprised that she had disliked it and had left so early. Instead, she stayed home, took care of her younger siblings, and learned how to tell stories and sew clothes expertly.

When I was 26, I asked my grandmother to retell me the folktales she had been telling for decades to both amuse and teach her grandchildren. Busia never reprimanded us, but instead told a story to impart the lesson. I once counted how many stories she told in the course of an ordinary day, and it added up to over 20. As a graduate student in Folklore, I was attempting to collect these tales, to record them. But now she, my beloved Busia, was facing a metal and mechanical cassette recorder instead of her flesh-and-blood grandchildren. There was no one to cheer when the wise man Krak defeated the dragon. No one to blush and giggle when she told the story of the boy named Little Fart. After a nervous pause, she leaned in to tell the mechanical beast and whoever might be listening the story of her life.

When she was 14, Wiktorya Migała's family decided to send her to America. As her Tata's favorite, she would fulfill his dream. Letters arrived from relatives in Chicago who invited her to live with them. Since she was so good at sewing, the relatives suggested that she could become a guest worker, sending her earnings back to her family. Yes, she would miss her family, but she would be back home in a year. Wiktorya, named after Queen Victoria, boarded the ship *Amerika* along with 999 other passengers. For someone who "didn't like the crowds," this was a challenge. She soothed herself with the knowledge that her father had planned to depart from this very same port a generation earlier.

At the Hamburg dock, a busy village had burgeoned, with takeaway eateries and beds for the night for the thousands of hopeful immigrants waiting to board. On the appointed day, Wiktorya headed toward the cramped steerage quarters where she would sleep, or tried to, in the top bunk in a windowless, congested room. She wore a tag safety-pinned to her blouse with her name and destination: Wiktorya Migała, Chicago. She was often seasick, lonely, and miserable but felt a sense of purpose. When she arrived at the port in New York on May 18, 1914, she spoke only Polish.

Although she had turned 15 by then, the clerk recorded her age as 17. Maybe she didn't understand the question. Or maybe she lied in order to be admitted to the country.

In Chicago, Wiktorya (now Victoria) moved in with her auntie and uncle on West Division Street in the heart of "The Polish Triangle." By 1918, a reported 383,000 Polish Americans lived in Chicago. The tight housing situation meant that an average of six people lived in each room, giving a person approximately 2 square yards of floor space. Enough room to lie down and sleep if you shared a bed.

My grandmother told me with pride that she had worked as a "tailor." She never said "seamstress" or "sewer." When I was a child, she sewed me beautiful clothes with exact replicas crafted for my dolls, right down to the trim on their dresses and the lining in their coats. Even when I was in college, she shortened my dresses repeatedly to fit the mini-skirt craze, and crocheted caps and scarves to keep me warm. But, in the early days of her time in the USA, she did her sewing in a sweatshop. In the hurry to complete work quickly, she lost three of her fingers to a machine.

Busia was supposed to stay in America for a year, but World War I broke out just months after her arrival and she was not allowed to return home. She met my grandfather and stayed a lifetime.

In the Limelight

From my grandmother's album. I'm guessing these are actors from my grandfather's acting troupe.

THE RING

My grandfather produced fake Polish weddings. Guests paid to attend the elaborate festivities for which Polish weddings were famous. Except his productions weren't the real deal. Instead, actors played the parts of bride and groom, bridesmaids, and ushers. Guests purchased tickets to chat with members of the ersatz wedding party, to banquet at the long tables of roasted meats, rye bread, and vodka. Late in the evening, as was the custom in genuine Polish weddings, the matron of honor would remove the bride's veil and tie an apron around her waist. Guests would pin cradle money to the apron in exchange for a dance with the make-believe bride. A live polka band played, and attendees enjoyed exuberant twirling, group singing, and memories of the Old Country.

In 1985, an off-Broadway show called *Tony and Tina's Wedding,* billed as "immersive theatre," became a hit and ran for 15 years. My grandfather's show was the Chicago version, except with polkas and pierogi. I like to think that my *dziadziu* was 70 years ahead of his time.

In the 1910s, theatrical productions were plentiful in Chicago's Polish Triangle. Comedies about immigrant characters making their way in the new country and dramas about the land they left were a frequent form of entertainment. Interestingly, almost every theatrical performance was followed by a ball. Chairs were cleared away and the audience joined the cast in dancing. My grandfather's mock Polish weddings fit local custom well.

Stanley (or Stashu as he was affectionately called) organized his theatrical weddings as fundraisers for his village back in Poland.

He had come to the U.S. as a guest worker to earn as much as he could for his impoverished hometown of Jadowniki Mokre, 37 miles east of Krakow. When World War I broke out, he could not return home as planned. But he continued to honor his mission not only with his earnings as a fruit-and-vegetable peddler, but with staged weddings, auctions, and raffles. He was clever and generous. And a very good dancer.

As my grandmother Victoria told the story, one day Stanley was going door-to-door in the old neighborhood, trying to raise money for his village by selling raffle tickets. When he knocked on the door at the Migała household, Victoria's auntie sent her to answer. Victoria had seen this boy before, with his peddler's horse and cart on Division Street. Her auntie had asked her to buy potatoes from him. And she recognized his pale blue eyes from when he spoke to the crowd at the reception hall just down the street from her building. She remembered how straight and proud he'd stood, telling his story not so different from her own. She also sent home every penny she could from her job, sewing clothes. He had come from a village not far from her own Dębica.

At her auntie's door, she listened to his pitch to buy a raffle ticket, calculated her funds, and bit her lower lip. She reached deep into her pocket for a few coins. Not wanting him to leave, and unsure of what to do next, she asked him a question. "What, please, is name of your horse? What is her name?"

He smiled and answered, "Henry. His name is Henry."

And they both enjoyed a little laugh.

When telling this story, my grandmother paused at this point. When she finally got up the nerve to speak, she blushed and said, "A week later, he came back, Stashu did. This time, instead of wearing cap and peddler's jacket, he was dressed like for the church with white starched collar but smelling like...like shirts left out in sunshine. He looked right at me with those terrible beautiful eyes. He told me I win prize! Me!! Prize! Ring, it was, this prize, with two stones. One white and one purple. I wanted to say something, to not look like dumbbell, so I asked, 'Please. What does it mean, the color of these stones?'

My maternal grandfather as a young man.

"And he knew. He said, 'The white, it stands for truth. And the purple, for love.' And then, he said 'So you see, it's true love.' He reached for my hand to put on this prize ring, but I tried to hide it. I didn't want him to see my bad fingers. But I didn't try so very hard, and he took it anyway and put the ring on one of my good fingers. He looked straight at my eyes and nodded his head a little."

My someday-grandmother Victoria, was a sensible girl of 17. Although she liked the way he smiled, she knew little about this boy, this Stashu. She would have to ask her auntie and uncle. And they answered yes, he was a good boy, and ambitious, knew how to raise money. This Kozial boy even spoke a little Greek and Yiddish too, from bargaining in the fruit-and-vegetable market. And, not to be forgotten, he owned a horse. They told her she would learn to love him.

And she did. Like her father, he played the concertina, and he was the best dancer in all of Chicago. Together, Stanley and Victoria opened a tiny grocery store in a basement, then a bigger one above ground. Stashu started to dabble in real estate, renovating and building houses. After some years, Stanley and Victoria moved to a stately home in the suburb of Norwood Park, where the neighbors at first snubbed them for their accents, their Catholicism, and their brood of children, but eventually came around to enjoy their warm company and generous hospitality. Together, my grandparents worked long hours and sang their hearts out. And whenever a girl married back in her hometown, Victoria sent the wedding dress.

*Later in life, my maternal grandparents celebrate
a family wedding.*

UPSTAIRS / DOWNSTAIRS at ST. STAN'S

My brother was an altar boy. He wore a long red cassock topped with a lace-trimmed surplice. He carried candles and banners in solemn processions. He helped set up the altar. He assisted at Mass. He filled cruets with water and wine and emptied them again into the priest's chalice. At home, over the dinner table, Richie sometimes snitched on which priests drank the most wine during the service. Nevertheless, when I saw him doing his altarly duties, I couldn't help but admire the ease with which he moved on the other side of the altar rail, where females weren't allowed to be, except to clean. Okay, I was jealous. There were no altar girls back then. And no female priests. He was part of a holy rite in a sacred space. A space that had awed me from an early age.

Our church was Baroque in style, graced with five altars. The ceilings were vaulted and embellished with elaborately painted angels, some playing harps or elongated trumpets, others singing. When I was very small, I spent many Masses looking up at the angels and whispering to them. I wanted to be like them, holy and pure, close to God. I tried not to look at the front altar with its painted triangle exhibiting a giant eye, signifying the all-seeing God. Did he really see me when I told my mother a lie about why I was late coming home from school, when I was actually watching *Howdy Doody* at Dennis Bara's basement apartment?

At each altar, statuary abounded. Jesus on the cross. Jesus descending from the cross. Jesus dying in his mother's arms. Saints galore with piercings and arrows and blood pouring through their sculpted robes. Drama, blood, and a lot of flesh for a spiritual setting. I miss it so.

Each day before school, we St. Stan's school children attended Mass. Yes, every single weekday we filed over 2-by-2 from the school, into the church, and into the pews. We went so often, I could recite the Latin Mass in my sleep. I might still be able to do it. *Introibo ad altare dei...* The nuns insisted we either follow the mass in the Daily Missal or read some other sanctioned holy book. After I had memorized the Latin Mass, I spent my time reading the New Testament. After I had read that several times, I went on to the hot, dramatic material in *The Lives of the Saints*. There, I could delight in being horrified by virgins having their eyes plucked out for not giving in to a pagan king's erotic advances. To my preteen self, this was titillating reading. Descriptions of lust, breasts, and blood were especially exciting reading when done inside the walls of the church. There, I often fantasized about being a virgin martyr myself, having my faith tested against the desires of the flesh. Along the way, I learned the symbols for dozens of saints, and this iconographical knowledge did come in handy in college Art History classes. And who knows, the saints' extraordinary stories might have contributed to my becoming a dramatist.

On Sundays, we all went to church again for a fancier, obligatory Honoring-God-on-the-Sabbath Mass. When I reached third grade, I started singing in the 9 a.m. children's choir. But I preferred attending the 12:15 Mass when the 100-voice adult choir was accompanied by a gigantic pipe organ. The sound was vast, and I loved being surrounded and permeated by it. Since our store closed at noon on Sunday, my family rushed liked crazy and often arrived late for that last, thunderous Mass where I sometimes thought I felt the presence of God.

My mother and other church ladies dance the can-can.

My mother danced the can-can in the church basement. She is on the far right in this photograph, next to Mrs. Lynch, sister-in-law to the pastor. The four dancers sewed their own costumes, and, in performance, showed a bit of leg. My mother loved every minute of it: the designing, rehearsal, and presentation. Nineteenth century can-can dancers were sometimes arrested for indecency but I'm sure the St. Stan's tantalizing production, billed as a fundraising event, was above reproach. The community gave a similar exemption to the performances of our neighborhood drag queen who earned only the highest praise. "What a performer!" "How convincing!" "What talent!"

*Our neighborhood drag queen performing as Sophie Tucker
in St. Stan's church basement.*

On the same church-basement stage, we children performed music and traditional Polish dances, such as the Krakowiak, in full folk costume. The boys wore boots and ballooning pants. We girls wore embroidered velvet vests and beribboned headdresses. I often had the fantasy that everyone else would forget their steps and abandon the stage. Only I would be left to save the day with a grand solo performance. Fortunately, it never happened. If it had, I suspect I would have faltered, fallen, or run off the stage. In a sixth-grade band concert, when featured in a flute duet, I suffered a fit of terrific nervousness and made a complete botch of my part. I played random notes that had nothing to do with what was on the score. My duet partner looked at me with horror. The church hall was full of neighbors and a slew of my relatives were in attendance. Although my mother's and Aunt Helene's faces showed concern, not one of my family ever commented on my failure. Ever. I believe that experience led me to realize that I was not a born performer and was happier off stage, writing.

The church basement events often included, you guessed it, food. It was a Polish parish, after all. Some performances were preceded or followed by a banquet with white tablecloths, servers, and generous portions served family style. Others involved attendees waiting in a cafeteria-style line for more casual food. Women in housedresses with their hair up in hairnets served "Polish hamburgers" made of ground meats mixed with breadcrumbs and onions and kept warm in copious amounts of gravy. I loved them in their tender sloppiness. I wish I had the recipe.

Centered on the church and its school, our area of Chicago resembled a village in Poland. Everyone knew everyone. You could never get lost. There was always someone to help if you needed it. It was like a Polish village, but with drag queens and can-can girls.

As I write this, I find myself saddened by the loss of St. Stan's as a community center and lively hub of activity. In the last few years, the Chicago Archdiocese has responded to lowered church attendance by consolidating parishes. St. Stanislaus parish has been merged with St. Genevieve's, where all church services and activities will be held. The physical church building of St. Stanislaus, Bishop & Martyr, has been shuttered.

MISS GLORIA

My childhood ballet teacher was a short, olive-skinned woman with a thicket of unruly black hair, a curvy body, and a magnetic smile. Miss Gloria didn't look like a classical ballerina but to me she was Anna Pavlova. Every Saturday morning, Miss Gloria Spranzo opened her storefront studio with its mirrored wall, hardwood floors, and upright piano to her adoring Polish and Italian-American students. Back at the bakery, my mother and aunties were hurriedly tossing buttercrust rolls into paper bags, while I danced to Debussy's *Clair de Lune* and moved into what I thought was the most elegant shape a human body could make: the arabesque.

The day Miss Gloria pronounced me ready for toe shoes, I nearly swooned. A few days later, my mother drove me downtown to a specialty store on the 14th floor of a warehouse-style building, carrying handwritten instructions from Miss Gloria as to style number and expected discount. I had been waiting for this moment for months. I aspired to the elegance of the satin slippers, the way the pink ribbons crossed on a ballerina's legs. Waiting on us was a gruff, balding salesman who stuffed a clump of lambswool into each pointe shoe, pushed my long-toed feet into the slippers, and hastily tied the slippery ribbons up my calves. And there they were, on my very own feet. I was too excited to take a step. I was in love. On the way home in the car, I petted my new toe shoes as if they were puppies.

After I had a few *en pointe* lessons from Miss Gloria, my mother gathered the family in our living room. Dad sat uncomfortably in his dress shoes. My brother held aloft a flashlight from behind the couch, shining it like a spotlight. Mom carefully situated the needle on her Swan Lake LP. I rose *en pointe* and stuttered across the linoleum with my arms raised like parentheses above my head. I improvised to the music and quickly took an exaggerated bow. My family applauded. For several weeks, we continued to gather for these amateur chamber performances. I gained confidence and let the music speak to me in longer and longer segments until baseball called to my brother and the family scattered.

Moving to music brought me joy and I wanted more. I signed up for every class Miss Gloria offered. I'll admit I was a clumsy failure at tumbling, but I enthused over the exuberance of tap, enjoyed the high kicks in chorus line, snapped my fingers in Calypso, and had fun swaying my hips in Hawaiian in spite of our orange glow-in-the-dark halter tops and yellow cellophane grass skirts.

*Pre-show photo of Miss Gloria's Calypso class with me
smiling widely on the right.*

Annually, Miss Gloria and her students did a public performance at the Lane Tech High School auditorium. In preparation, my mom smeared an abundance of rouge on my cheeks and transformed my hair into Shirley Temple locks with a hot curling iron. From the wings, I watched Miss Gloria perform her solos with elegance and grace. Inspired, I stepped onto the stage.

When we were teenagers, my cousin Wally and I danced together like Fred and Ginger. Or so our mothers, who were sisters, told us. At family weddings and anniversaries, we waltzed and fox-trotted. But we especially enjoyed showing off our jitterbug. In one move, Wally held me by my waist, slid me between his feet, then quickly lifted me up above his head, and bounced me on each of his knees before putting me down. We whirled, we twirled. We shimmied and shook.

Other evenings, often spent at my house playing an LP of *West Side Story*, we danced and sang the entire score. We knew every word and acted all the parts. We finished with a slow hand-in-hand march to "There's a Place for Us," inspiring our trapped audience of grandparents, aunts, uncles and cousins to shed a tear and applaud. One night Wally changed the record, and we pretended to know how to tango. We had seen it in a movie. We set our faces in haughty poses and performed several dramatic crosses. On an overly quick turn, I kicked up my leg extra high while he scooped his arm down and, instead of encircling my waist, his hand landed on my privates. We both yelped and jumped apart. Wally apologized profusely and we broke out in embarrassed laughter.

During my early years at the University of Miami, I attended plenty of social dances, but I had no dance teacher or regular partner. I was missing an integral part of my self-expression. Some evenings,

I let myself into the empty sorority social hall and played Barbra Streisand, blasting the sound system, and belting out the songs. I moved across the floor, letting the music take over. In my teens and early twenties, this is how I dealt with strong emotion. Main squeeze seen with another woman? Confusion over the existence of God? I coped by dancing to "People" and "Don't Rain on My Parade." Whatever the upset, I leaned into it, moved to it, found my way through it. Interpretative dance saved my sanity.

———

When I was 23, a visitor arrived at my airshaft apartment on West 111th Street in New York. To create a cool ambience, I had painted the wall panels in imitation of Adolph Gottlieb and sewn a Good Will fur coat over a chair. Posters from the contemporary art gallery where I worked covered the bathroom walls. The visitor was a friend of an ex-boyfriend, and he was carrying a flute. He strolled in and immediately started playing. I listened for a bit and started to move. I danced barefoot around the living room, feeling the rhythm, the intensity, the surges, and pauses. We dueted for an hour or so. When he stopped playing, I turned toward him with what my mother would have called a "come hither" look. He shook his head and said, "We already made love." With a quiet smile, he left my apartment.

———

I had to be in my 40s when my dear, but much younger friend Georg'Ann suggested that she and I sign up for a tapdancing class. This impulse was not completely out of the blue. In our social group it was customary to dance after dinner, often to our newly discovered Brazilian samba tunes. Plus, Georg'Ann and I had attended numerous dance concerts together and, when big name troupes came through town to perform at the university, we often signed up for the Master Classes.

So, when Georg'Ann suggested tapdancing, I was primed. We

acquired shiny patent leather shoes with Cuban heels. We faithfully attended classes in an upstairs studio on the town square and I remembered blissful days at Miss Gloria's. Sometimes we practiced our time step on the sidewalk that connected our two houses. Stomp, hop, step, flap, ball change. When time came for a public performance, a grad student friend of Georg'Ann's, a Brit named Stephen, said he was going to be there. Oh, no! An actual audience? Georg'Ann assured me that Stephen had a good sense of humor. Not far into the program, I performed an enthusiastic stomp with extra vigor and knocked the heel off one of my shoes. I limped along through the rest of the program, marking the last chapter of my tapdancing career.

―――――

As a senior woman, I take an aqua exercise class with my friend Jeffrey Ann. As part of the routine, the teacher instructs all the women who are floating with the help of brightly colored foam noodles to kick one leg up out of the water, eight times. I have longish legs and have remained flexible enough to lift a leg high and touch my knee to my nose. In class, I do the move quickly and, for fun, add the extra touch of pointing my (now arthritic) toe. Every time new people in the class see this kick, they exclaim their surprise and I always reply, "I used to be a Rockette!" I usually get a "Wow!" or "Really?" in response and then I come clean. Except sometimes I don't.

―――――

At home most mornings, after some yoga stretches and exercises, I let myself move to melody. My movement is limited by age, but I allow the music to take over my body. I enjoy swirling my arms and leaning down to graze the floor with my fingertips. I slide across the floor. Sometimes, I recall how a tiny studio in an immigrant neighborhood brought me such delight and I silently thank Miss Gloria for helping give shape to my passionate flailing, encouragement to my budding artistry. And, on lucky days, I move on and lose myself in the rhythm of writing. My fingers dance across the keys. I become part of the music of words, move into the flow of the piece. Experience pleasure. Passion. Movement. Life.

MY GAY FIANCE

Bob and me in his New York City apartment.

My gay boyfriend Bob asked me to marry him. We spent an afternoon on New York's 5th Avenue pretending we were rich people shopping for an engagement ring. At Cartier's, we picked out a multi-tiered ring loaded with diamonds and emeralds that weighed a few pounds. The salesman escorted us to the back room so I could see how lovely the ring looked on the full-length me in their 3-way mirror. I exclaimed how I LOVED the ring and Bob would comment how he thought the green of the emeralds brought out my eyes. We went on to Tiffany's to comparison shop, laughing all the way. It was a fake engagement, and we were pretending, playing parts. We got a kick out of this kind of thing, pretending we were people we were not: Broadway actors, interior decorators.

Bob and I had known each other since childhood. He'd grown up in the Italian neighborhood next door to our Polish one. In high school, he was my cousin Wally's best friend. Bob and I had co-directed and choreographed a community-theatre production of *A Connecticut Yankee in King Arthur's Court*. We co-wrote a so-so play entitled *Someday*. We played around with an opera we called *French Toast,* performing its duet while preparing breakfast.

Somewhere along the line, we accidentally fell in love. When we lived apart after I moved to New York, we sent each other love letters. His were written on music paper that included bits of compositions he dedicated to me. Once he moved to New York, Bob walked 20 blocks and up five flights of stairs most nights to join me for dinner. Afterwards, we'd sit on the bench of the baby grand piano in my shared sublet apartment and sing the scores of musicals. We especially favored the score of "The Fantasticks," which we had seen during its record-breaking New York run.

I went to the Tony Awards on his arm. True, we had to get out of a taxi a few blocks away since we couldn't afford a limo. And true, he only had tickets because he was a rehearsal pianist for a nominated show, which meant our seats were as far from the stage as you could climb. Still, it was fun listening to the fans assembled alongside the red carpet trying to guess who we were as we walked the red carpet. Carol Lynley? That blonde from *Hair*? Was he…Pacino, maybe?

But, in reality, I was a college student who aspired to be a full-time writer and he was a church organist and rehearsal pianist who aspired to be a full-time composer, and we really really wanted to write a musical of our own. In those days everyone we knew carried around packs of Marlboros or Salems in their handbags and jacket pockets. And we loved the Art Deco style of the Prohibition Era. So we came up with an idea for a musical forecasting an era of cigarette prohibition. We called it "The Smoldering Seventies." Yes, this was a long, long, long time ago in the 1960s when the Seventies were still ahead of us. We named one of the lead characters "Puffy," a hot nightclub singer at one of the "smoke-easies." While Bob and I sang Puffy's solo from the baby grand, my roommate, Xenia, slowly and sultrily pulled off her dishwashing gloves in the adjoining kitchen, tossing them into the sink with a sexy shrug of her shoulders. The song was titled, "They Call Me 'Puffy' but My Name is 'The Flame'." A dusty copy of the score sits in my writing room to this day. We never tried to sell it because we didn't know how. We didn't know where to begin.

My gay boyfriend asked me to marry him. I was in my cap and gown, just about to graduate from Barnard, my mother had just arrived in New York City to watch me walk, and I was madly in love with him. Not that he gave me a ring. But he promised me one and I was thrilled.

When my Barnard classmates found out he had proposed, they surrounded me and cheered. Even though Barnard was a college renowned for its highly capable and intellectual female students, there was a lingering sense of tradition that one should get engaged at one's graduation.

Bob and me on my Barnard graduation day, newly engaged.

This time we weren't play-acting at Tiffany's. Bob had been the love of my life for years. And it wasn't that I didn't have other possibilities. One particular Columbia student made a project of proposing to me every day for a hundred days. Another suitor came to me the night before he married someone else to give me one last chance to accept him. Blond, wholesome, Midwestern looks were in vogue at the time, and I had, so I was told, "good child-bearing hips."

My mother was thrilled with the engagement news. He knew how to play the piano. He had gone to high school with my brother. I had been a bridesmaid at his sister's wedding. Mom thought maybe the two of us would move back to Chicago and raise her grandkids nearby. We clearly loved each other madly and spent every evening together. What could go wrong? She and my grandmother set out to buy us a set of Grande Baroque silver as an engagement present. I still have it today.

What Mom didn't know, but maybe suspected, was the part about Bob's being gay. I myself actively pushed the knowledge away. Although we didn't have sex very often, we had hours-long make-out sessions. Bob once suggested we enter a contest for the longest kiss because he really thought we'd win. Later, I found out that, after these long arousing sessions, Bob would secretly go to a bar and pick up a guy for real sex. Nonetheless, we declared our love for each other often and he kept promising me a ring.

The engagement diamond never came. Bob postponed and postponed the wedding. He started getting regular visits from one particular guy from back home in Chicago. One night, visiting Bob's apartment, I saw the words "I love you" written in the dust on Bob's stovetop range hood. We had to acknowledge the truth. He was in love with a man. I started hearing stories about the baths and bars where a guy could pick up another guy and go have sex with him right upstairs. I learned more than I wanted to know. We tried hard, had some bad, painful sex. By Thanksgiving, it was over.

Decades later, I wrote about this highly romantic unworkable relationship in my play *Dear John.* I sent it to Bob who was living in Los Angeles at the time, and he wrote back, "I read it 24 times! I LOVE IT!!"

Robert DeChristopher at the piano.

Another decade later, when my now husband Tom and I were spending a year in the Los Angeles area, I gave Bob a call. As soon as he heard my voice, he cried out, "Marcia!" He invited Tom and me to attend an Easter Mass in West Hollywood dedicated to the memory of those lost to AIDS. Robert DeChristopher was conducting the orchestra and chorus. The congregation, comprised mostly of gay men, spent a great deal of the service turned toward the choir loft to better enjoy the jubilant music of resurrection. I felt proud. The friendship continued.

THE RACE

*My cousins Mietek and Bruno with me on the
castle hill in Krakow.*

M y cousin Bruno raced his car, trying to beat the train. My
visa was expiring at midnight. The rules during the
Communist regime were strict and the tension palpable.
Bruno's face and knuckles were white. It was all my fault. Unused
to European schedules, I had misread the time of my train's

departure. My ticket read 18:00. Somehow, I had managed to skip a digit and thought I was leaving at 8 p.m. I was departing from Poland for the country then called Czechoslovakia after several weeks spent with Bruno and his family. Because of my mistake, I had barely missed the train as it departed. Bruno thought he could catch up with it before the next stop. Or the one after that. He was literally racing his car alongside the train.

I had met Bruno in Chicago one evening at the home of a distant cousin. Family told us we were related, though we never could figure out exactly how. Bruno had come to the U.S. as a guest worker, much as my grandparents had decades before. His wife Wanda and their children remained behind in Nowy Targ for two years while Bruno worked to make their future more secure. In Chicago, Bruno learned English or what he thought was English, from his Great-Aunt Stefcha, who instead of "car," said *"machina"* for this vehicle invented, or at least popularized, after her own immigration. In Polish the word is *"samochod."* Bruno ended up speaking a tongue neither Polish nor English.

In a mishmash of languages—English, Polish, and Polish-Chicagoan—he and I managed to communicate and have a good laugh. At the end of the evening, Bruno invited me to come visit him and his family in Nowy Targ.

Three years later, I did, along with two friends. The first surprise was that Bruno owned a *cukiernia,* a bakery, as had my immediate family. The second was that we arrived before my letter announcing our visit, so no one knew we were coming. Nonetheless, the family opened their home to the three hippies at their door. Bruno took off from work and gave us tours of the surrounding area. The third surprise was seeing men in embroidered white woolen outfits digging ditches and leading sheep through fields. They were doing manual labor in what I thought of as holiday folk costumes.

*My friends Richard and Jeanne and me having fun
up in the Tatra Mountains.*

Bruno took us to nearby Zakopane, a popular ski town where even more local people wore similar Gorale folk costumes while performing everyday activities. My friends and I were enthralled. We bought tourist goods of tooled leather and carved wood. I bought an embroidered blouse and vest for myself. As we ascended on a ski lift, we looked out a window to see an elderly mountaineer woman in a babushka stomping through the snow, making better time than we were. Bruno took us to yet another town, Chochołów, where the Alpine-style houses were carved of light-hued wood, a folk village where people rode in wagons and sleighs. The hillsides were covered in the kind of haystacks I had only previously seen in 19th-century paintings.

After my friends left, Bruno's brother, Mietek, took me to see Warsaw and other Polish cities, followed by two weeks in my cousins' mountain apartment.

Mietek and me in the town square of Krakow.

But now my time was up, my visa expiring. When it was clear Bruno was not going to catch up with the train, he took a deep breath and changed direction, driving to a border in the mountains. With minutes left on my visa, I listened as he instructed me to walk down a path through the woods and over a bridge. I nodded, hugged him goodbye, hefted my leather mail bag over my shoulder, and picked up my large yellow suitcase. He waved me on, telling me to hurry. I reminded myself that the last thing I wanted was a stay in a Soviet jail.

As I started walking down the path and onto a footbridge, the world turned black and white. I was suddenly in an old spy movie full of suspense and mystery, surrounded by dense woods, making it impossible to see on either side, much less ahead. After walking half a mile or so, I spied ahead a small booth occupied by a solitary guard. He carefully investigated my papers and my face. After an uncomfortably long pause and a re-examination of documents, he finally stamped my visa and handed everything back to me. Relieved, I continued walking. Soon, I found myself in a pitch-dark

Czech village. It was after midnight. Clearly, everyone was asleep. I dropped my bags in the middle of a street and cried out, "Where am I?" No one answered. I continued walking until I saw far-off lights and headed toward them. A train station! Hallelujah!

I boarded a train to Prague. Seated in my compartment were two smiling men who tried to converse with me. Their Czech sounded a little like Polish and my pocket dictionary helped me to decipher what they were trying to say, which was a version of "Guess what we do." Ah, we were going to play "What's My Line?" Looking for occupational hints from their faces and clothes, I couldn't help but notice the black outlines around their eyes, like heavy eyeliner. The first thought I had was that they were drag queens. I thought better of saying this and gave up the game. I shrugged my shoulders. I put a quizzical look on my face. Finally, one of them spoke up. "Coal miners." That was coal dust around their eyes. They smiled and pointed to the mountains around us where they worked. Like many people I would meet on European trains, these two men were eager to make friends, even through language barriers.

I would visit Bruno and his family again, with each of my husbands, once pregnant, and then with my grown daughter. Each time, Bruno dropped what he was doing and took us on a variety of elaborate day tours to see the land of my foremothers and forefathers. At the end, he always pulled out a bottle of vodka. The common wisdom was that once you opened a bottle, you had to drink until it was empty. Of course, platters of food appeared. Repeatedly, I was impressed by the hospitality of these relatives I barely knew. Generous hospitality I would one day try to capture in my own fiction, drama, and home.

The American Dream

The story of
my grandparents'
rise and fall

1917–1930

Told in Pictures

My grandfather with his grocery delivery wagon
and horse, Henry.

My grandparents' "Grocery and Candies" store in a basement.
They lived in an apartment above.

My grandfather behind the counter of his store.

My maternal grandparents behind the counter of a bigger grocery store. Over the years, my grandfather learned to be a meat cutter as well.

After some years of flipping houses, my grandfather started investing in new construction. The girl likely is my mother, who helped him put up wallpaper from a very young age.

My grandparents, their children, and visitors at their Norwood Park home. At that time, my grandfather didn't bother counting one-dollar bills, preferring instead to stuff them into jars.

During the stock market crash of 1929 my grandparents lost all their money. They were forced to move back to the tenements, into a cold-water flat. The flags in this photo suggest the 4th of July.

Home

and

Away

THE VASE

My grandmother had one dollar left. She had counted up the nickels, dimes, and pennies and that's all she had. One hundred cents. And, at the time, five children to feed. Gone were the days when her husband Stashu couldn't be bothered counting dollar bills. He used to shove them into jars he stored in the basement of their stately Norwood Park home. Gone were the days when she could buy crystal vases and fancy dresses. She remembered how a salesman had once come to the house and showed her elegant clothes. He encouraged her to try on a dress adorned with tiny seed pearls and handmade lace that cost a hundred dollars, telling her that she deserved it, that she worked hard. She bought it and wore it to a dance. It fit her just so. The women admired her and Stashu was proud.

But now, after climbing the American Dream ladder from peddler to groceryman to real estate investor, her Stashu lost everything in the Great Depression. They had to declare bankruptcy. They had to sell everything—house, car, furniture, children's toys, paintings, dresses, vases—everything, and move back to the tenement neighborhood where they had started out as peddler and sweatshop worker. Except now they had no jobs. No one was hiring. They lived in a basement apartment, a cold water flat. They were down to their last dollar.

Victoria put her oldest daughter Kazia (my mother, a.k.a. Casey, Casmira) in charge of the younger children and went out with her handful of change. Victoria remembered her own childhood in Poland, how she had always been hungry. How her mother had told her to be proud that they were a family with two bowls when most of the villagers had just one. Two bowls. One for the parents and one for the children. She remembered making tunnels through the mashed potatoes in the large bowl, laughing along with her brothers and sisters, her mother telling them not to play with their food. They had eaten potatoes almost every night for dinner. On feast days, they had delighted in sausages with purple horseradish and braided bread dotted with raisins. Some days, there was no food at all. One day, all her mother could put on the table was a tin can filled with wildflowers she had stolen from the forest.

Victoria thought of her own meager patch of flowers, dug up from her Norwood Park house gardens and replanted in large tin cans emptied of sauerkraut. Despite objections from Stashu, she clung to this last gasp of beauty from their previous life. She turned to look at them just in time to see one of the many stray dogs of the neighborhood lift his leg to water her flowers. She stamped and shooed the dog away, surprised at her own anger and loud voice.

She tried to concentrate on what she might be able to buy at the grocer's. A soupbone? A few turnips if she was lucky. She herself never sat down at the table to eat. She served her husband and children. She stood and ladled soup into bowls. She spooned mashed potatoes into small mouths. She always ate after everyone else and only what her husband and children had left on their plates. She managed on leftovers. She managed.

Victoria decided to walk down Division Street to the grocery, so she could pass the pawn shop window. She liked to look at the gold pocket watches and shiny accordians, the china dolls and painted dishes from lives gone by. She liked to see if she could spot any new items in the shop window. And then she saw it. A cut crystal vase that caught the light and broke it into tiny rainbows. It resembled one that she had once had herself. She couldn't help herself. She went in to have a closer look, to hold it in her hand. To admire a bit of beauty in those hard times.

The shop owner told her she had a good eye. Made in Poland by the best of craftsmen. But the price was a firm five dollars.

Victoria spilled out the change from her cloth bag on the counter, pleaded and bargained with the shop owner. Repeatedly, he shook his head no. She grew silent. Stood still. Stayed still until the shopkeeper's resolve wore thin.

Victoria walked back to her building and harvested the flowers she had managed to keep alive in rusty cans on the stoop. Larkspur. Columbine. Marigolds. She unwrapped the vase, washed it carefully, and held it to the light, letting the colors dance on the walls. She filled the vase with water from the pump at the sink, trimmed the stems and added the blossoms. She spread out her shawl as a kind of tablecloth and centered the arrangement. She looked at it from different angles. Quietly, she hummed. She called the children in from playing in the alley. Kazia, Helcia, Joey, Wally, and Dolores. She called Stashu in from pacing the sidewalk.

They sat down at the table and held hands to say Grace.

That night, they feasted on beauty alone.

PINK NEON

*A neighbor girl, my brother Rich, and me on the
front steps of the family bakery.*

My father named the family bakery after my mom. Her given first name was "Casmira" and she was called "Kazia" by her Polish family. But among Americans, she was "Casey." A pink neon sign reading "Casey's Pastry Shop" hung in a large glass window facing our residential street, Lotus Avenue. If you were to walk into the bakery's front door, you'd face glass counters full of poppyseed cakes, Kaiser and buttercrust rolls, apple pies and Polish cheesecakes. Against the wall were wooden shelves covered in paper doilies, showing off rye, wheat, and pumpernickel loaves, and braided raisin breads, all filling the bakery with a glorious just-baked fragrance. Or so I'm told. Those of us who lived with the constant aroma of baking couldn't smell a thing unless it was burning.

A refrigerated case exhibited strawberry shortcakes and pastry horns filled with whipped cream. Aproned women would welcome you with smiles and ask you to please take a number. These women packaged cakes into white cardboard boxes which they tied up with string, finishing with a bow. To slice bread, they used a frightening-looking sharp machine. They rang up transactions on a venerable old cash register. During slow times, I was sometimes allowed to stand on a chair and push down the keys that finalized sales.

My mother trained her help always to be welcoming and friendly. A sign facing the saleswomen behind the counter read, "It takes fewer muscles to smile than to frown." The bakery was popular, and a line often formed outside the door by 6 a.m.

If you happened to be a child of the owners, lucky like me, you could scoot behind the counter and filch a handful of cookies to treat your jealous friends. And, let's say, instead of helping yourself to treats, you were to walk through the door behind the counter, to the right of the bread-slicing machine, you would find yourself in an eat-in kitchen with a stove almost always in use making chicken soup or oxtail stew for the bakers, and also a sink, a dog, a bird, and a telephone.

Everyone answered the phone with a singsong, "Casey's Pastry Shop," for the kitchen was also the business office. During the day, my mother conducted meetings at the Formica table with representatives of companies who sold apricot preserves, poppy seeds, yeast, flour, and insurance. A bottle of whiskey often appeared at such meetings. My mother believed in being hospitable and greasing wheels to get a good deal. Late at night, my mother sat at the same table, making entries in her ledgers. During slow times, the door to the kitchen was left open and the store help would chat with the family. I recall coming home from shopping with my mother and showing the shopgirls my first garter belt, acquired to hold up the stockings under my first Holy Communion dress. The women who worked in the store were both my literal and ersatz aunties.

A glass door with a lace curtain led to the private areas of the house. The living room was furnished with a couch, a hand-carved coffee table (which I have to this day), and an easy chair. A spinet piano where my mother played Chopin and a 3-foot-high polished wooden radio provided entertainment. Stacks of *Glamour* and *Good Housekeeping* magazines were piled on the radiators behind the couch. An arched cove next to the easy chair housed *Reader's Digest* condensed books and *Book of Knowledge* encyclopedia volumes. These tomes hid the family safe.

The constant presence of white flour dust in the bakery made carpeting impossible so my mother chose a gray linoleum for the floor in a swirly, carpet-like pattern. Personally, I thought it a little shiny for carpeting, but I never said that out loud. A large print of flamingoes graced one of the walls.

Separating the living room and my parents' bedroom was a large archway. Offering a small measure of privacy between the two rooms was a folding screen wallpapered in a pattern of exotic, jungle foliage, echoing the theme of a print in the living room. Mom's parakeet Skippy often perched on the screen, maybe drawn by the large leaves and colorful flowers.

Religious pictures and crucifixes adorned my parents' bedroom which featured a gray bedroom set, including a large dresser displaying vials of cologne and makeup that I liked to play with. If you were to turn left, you'd find a small windowless room where I slept and napped as a toddler, within easy earshot of my mother and the aunties who worked in the store.

My brother had another windowless bedroom off the kitchen hallway. After my father made us a new bedroom up in the attic, both of our old bedrooms became storage areas where my brother and I often played. We had a horseracing boardgame, checkers, cards, and jacks. Sometimes we took turns pretending to be a priest, raising an aluminum wine glass above our heads and making pronouncements in Latin. My brother was an altar boy, so he knew his *Dominus Vobiscum*s.

Down the hall, on your right, a short hallway led to the bathroom with its clawed-foot tub. This small facility was shared by our 4-member family and the store help. Between the hall and the bath was a stairway to the attic.

When I was around seven or eight, my parents remodeled half of the attic into a bedroom/rec room where my brother, myself, and, for a couple of years, my grandmother slept. The other half of the attic housed a lot of forgotten junk and a ping pong table. The attic had an outside door to a tarpaper-covered rooftop where, on her rare days off, my mother and I would sunbathe. My mother often issued warnings not to walk too close to the edge of the roof since it lacked any railings. I recently looked up a listing for the building and noticed that this outside area has been updated with railings and elaborate outdoor furniture featuring umbrellaed tables. It's no longer a bakery, after all. The building now features apartments and is listed for $478,000.

On the first floor, a long hallway extended from the shop, where the baked goods were baked, to the store where the baked goods were sold. My mom and her assistants carried heavy trays of birthday cakes and apple pies through this passageway which was lined with shelves and stacks of bakery supplies. The plentitude of plastic swans, columns, candies, and ribbons stored in this hallway delighted me as a child Plus, there were cardboard boxes full of edible flowers and grownup dolls with shapely figures. My father would stand such dolls in the middle of skirt-shaped cakes which he frosted and decorated for Sweet-Sixteen parties.

The bakery shop was another country. Peopled by strong men with bare arms in long white aprons, the huge room groaned with the sounds of giant mixers and Polish expletives. The focus, the eye of the room, was the gaping red maw of a hot brick oven. Men shoveled bread and cake dough into the oven on huge paddles and shoveled them out again to be put on cooling racks that were twice my height. Freezers and refrigerators lined one wall. The room had its own exterior door and a half bath I dared not enter as a child. A sneak peek inside revealed layers of dirty flour over the grime of a rarely cleaned restroom. My mother never ventured there.

On the other side of the shop was a garage that served as storage for 100-pound bags of flour, 5-gallon metal tubs of raspberry jam, and huge boxes of bananas. The latter were sometimes home to leggy creatures we'd call "banana spiders," commonly known as tarantulas, that occasionally escaped into the house. A second garage always housed the latest model of a Buick Roadmaster.

If you exited the bakery shop into the world, you found yourself on a cement yard, where the neighborhood youth gathered to play Kick the Can. We kids hid behind trash barrels in the adjoining alley, sneaking out to kick a tin can to win.

When my brother became a teen, he acquired a hoop that turned the cement yard into a basketball court. I liked to hang around and watch the older boys play, so I fed them snacks. After my brother was rushed to the hospital with an appendicitis attack, he blamed me because he thought I had fed him too many dried apricots on the basketball court.

Trying to remember the layout of the house and bakery a few days ago, I left a message for my cousin Wally, who had grown up a few blocks away. When Wally called me back, he said, "I've drawn up a floor plan!" I said, "Me, too!" We eagerly compared notes. Our memories coincided. We could both see the pink neon "Casey's Pastries" sign still glowing in our minds' eyes.

POLISH EASTER

My Polish uncle threw a glassful of water at me. I had been innocently walking into the kitchen behind the *cukiernia* (bakery) in Nowy Targ on a Monday morning when— *whoosh!* The brand-new maternity blouse I had purchased in Copenhagen was streaked with wet, my face and hair were dripping. I yelped. But then I heard his laugh. It was a festive, gotcha! kind of laugh, and everyone in the kitchen giggled along with him. For the rest of the day, I saw people throwing water, surprising each other as they came around corners or through doors. It was Dyngus Day in Poland, a day-after-Easter custom that my family had forgotten to bring to America.

Bill, my first husband, and I had come to Poland so that I could experience Polish Easter firsthand. Throughout my childhood, Easter had been the most important holiday of the year. We fasted for 40 days looking forward to it, giving up chocolate or lollipops or movies, suffering in anticipation of the glorious feast of rebirth. The week before Easter, we visited Polish churches in Chicago where all the statuary was draped in purple. Sorry for our sins of the previous year, we put our knees to the hard floors and walked painfully up the church aisles. We gathered to prepare Easter food, grating our knuckles along with red beets to flavor the fresh horseradish we made. Our home smelled of just-made white sausage, a fresh kielbasa stuffed and flavored by my maternal grandfather from pork raised by my Uncle Dravis. We dyed and painted eggs. We carved lambs out of butter.

On Good Friday, we spent from noon to 3 p.m. in silence without even the company of music. We were reputedly contemplating the suffering of Christ on the cross, but I wasn't very good at it. I tended to sneak in some reading and radio. My father baked dozens of Easter lamb cakes. I looked longingly at the ones frosted with chocolate icing and raisins for eyes.

On Holy Saturday came my favorite custom: the blessing of the Easter baskets. I'm not talking about the cellophane-wrapped, confection-filled versions sold at drugstores for children, though those could be blessed as well. I'm recalling the special rectangular basket we kept for Easter, which we lined with a freshly laundered and ironed, lace-trimmed and nun-embroidered napkin, then filled with samples of our Easter meals to come: decorated eggs, sausages, ham, slices of rye and pumpernickel, little jars of plain and beet horseradish, cellars of salt and pepper, a butter lamb. To our Lent-starved selves, the food smelled better than any other.

A butter lamb from last year's Easter.

We carried the covered baskets to the church basement where we placed them on a waiting table. A young priest entered, wearing a white surplice and stole, carrying a wand of holy water. We lifted the embroidered cloth to let the holiness rain on our food and then rushed home to eat the first Easter meal, Holy Saturday lunch. No food tasted better than the newly blessed, newly permitted meats and eggs. We wished each other *Wesołego Alleluja* and plunged in. Ah, the glory of that first bite of sausage with nose-prickling horseradish. From the stove, my mother ladled out bowls of newly made beet-red *barszcz*.

Easter Day demanded a new dress and, yes, an Easter bonnet. The church was always crowded with those too lazy to attend the rest of the year. But the glorious music, the choir singing jubilantly made us glad to see everyone and filled our hearts with the promise of spring and a new start on life. Christ had risen. So, why couldn't we? My parents were snappy dressers, and this was a day to strut their stuff. Then, home to an Easter meal of baked ham, salads and asparagus, the special Easter rye, more colored eggs and, yes, the lambs carved out of butter.

With great anticipation, I had planned the trip to Poland to soak up the European sources of all that color, aroma, and spirit. Bill and I were living in Copenhagen, just a 50-mile ferry ride from the coast of my ancestors' country. Besides, we had just acquired a bright yellow Volvo station wagon, which we had picked up straight from the factory in Sweden. Time to give it a whirl, take it on its first trip.

Poland was still behind the Iron Curtain at the time, so we had to fill out lengthy paperwork requesting entry. We had to exchange a hefty amount of money in advance. Approved, funds deposited, we set off toward our destination. At the passport check, officials in menacing uniforms told us we were missing one important document that showed our having exchanged the money. We argued that we wouldn't have gotten visas without it. Nonetheless, we had to exchange more funds at the border. All our cash for hotels and restaurants and gifts went into the second exchange and we were forced to stay in hotels with straw mattresses and to eat in humble eateries, but we moved on. When we wakened each morning, our shiny new car was surrounded by a crowd of admirers. No one had ever seen its likes before.

Our first stop was Nowy Targ, to visit my cousin Bruno. Unfortunately, once again, the letter telling him of our approaching

Easter visit had never reached him and his face was filled with surprise when he saw us among the last-minute customers in his pastry shop. He led us inside where his parents scurried to find a bed for us. We had to make do with a single bed where workers took naps in the back room of the bakery. A 6-foot-tall man and a pregnant woman in a single bed did not make for a comfy night's sleep.

Then came the news that this branch of the family were sophisticated non-believers who did not attend church at all, not even on Easter. No horseradish. No butter lambs. No traditions. Bruno dutifully took us on tours of the local sites and his parents scrounged among their most precious possessions to give us a wedding gift. The gorgeous cut crystal bowl weighed a ton and probably cost them a year's income, but we had to accept. We had brought them a teapot of Royal Copenhagen china but it was hardly the same worth.

And then, it was Easter Monday and Bruno's dad was throwing water on me. Okay, we acquired one new custom out of our visit. Time to move on to another branch of the family. We drove through the hills to my grandmother's hometown of Dębica. We passed hand-carved churches in the mountains with steeples in the Eastern European style, resembling the bulbous towers one sees in pictures of Moscow. I decided on the spot that my last name, which literally means "onion-like," referred to this lovely shape.

My grandmother's family had been eagerly awaiting us for days. We were late. They had expected us for Easter itself, Holy Week even. Okay, good that my letter arrived here. Not good that something was lost in translation. We had missed church services and processions, tables heavy with newly blessed Easter food. We had missed the very reason for the trip.

"Never mind," they said, as they made up the tables and covered them with embroidered cloths and food. Easter cards greeted us at our places at the table. Hams and potatoes. Platters of vegetables. Horseradish and butter lambs. And there, among the babkas and other desserts, lambs made of sugar! The fiddles and concertinas came out. Happy songs were sung. While in graduate school, Bill had learned German. So had my grandmother's brother Franciszek during the days of the German occupation. And so, stories went around the table translated from English to Polish to German and back. Spirits were high. The feast moved from house to house. Every night, they cried to part with us; every morning, they sang to greet us again.

My pregnant belly was rubbed and blessed. My relatives asked who was going to take care of this child? I answered that I was, of course. "No, no," they said, "You can't do it alone. It is too much work!" I looked around at the children in the room, a baby being rocked by a disabled-auntie, a toddler on the knee of his grandfather. "It is 24-hour job! You must have help!" I thought about how I would be 500 miles away from my mother, my grandmother, my aunties and cousins. I pushed the thoughts from my mind, but they came back to me when I was a new mother juggling too much responsibility. In the immigration, what had we gained and what had we lost?

The relatives stood around the bright yellow car and marveled at our wealth. We offered to take an enthusiastic auntie for a ride. We took our places in the front seats and waited. She stood outside the back door. "Go, open the door for her, Bill. She's old school. Wants a man to open it for her." Bill scurried out and opened her door. When she was safely inside, she said, "I am so sorry. I did not know how to open door. So sorry."

Our bags packed with souvenirs and food for the road, our bellies and our hearts full of warmth and song, we set off on our return. I carried news to my grandmother about who looked good these days, and how well-behaved the children were, and who had built a house from the rubble of the war, and what we ate and what songs were sung. I brought her a sugar lamb.

HOT CHILI

My brother Rich and me in New Mexico.

My mother's cousin, "Aunt Sophie," was getting a divorce and moving to Albuquerque. We'd never heard of such a thing. We lived in a Catholic neighborhood dominated by the smokestack of a factory and the spires of a church. No one got divorced. Sophie was leaving "Uncle Charlie" because he had forced her to do certain sexual things that she did not want to do. She explained this to my mom within my six-year-old earshot. Aunt Sophie thought I should know about life.

I was sorry she was leaving. She and Uncle Charlie owned a paint store a block from our bakery. Sometimes, while she and my mom chatted, I got to play with paint chips, arranging and re-arranging the colors in various patterns.

A year after Sophie moved away, my mother, brother, and I took a train to visit her. I loved watching the changing landscape whiz by outside the window. I felt grown up and classy eating on white tablecloths in the dining car.

Once in New Mexico, we visited an Indian reservation where my mother bought a Native-patterned blanket I still have today. Aunt Sophie also took us to a Mexican restaurant with a tree growing inside. Inside! My mother, afraid that my tender taste buds would be outraged by green chili, ordered me a burger off the children's menu. My brother took one bite of his chili, got a horrified look on his face, then drank most of his water. Coughing, he offered to trade with me. I inhaled the exotic aroma and gladly accepted. This was the life. I swore I would return to Albuquerque when I grew up.

Years later, I visited Albuquerque with Tom, my second husband. Strolling around Old Town, I thought I recognized the restaurant. We read the menu and went in. When I told the waitress that I thought I might have eaten there 40 years earlier, she replied that she heard that a lot. The tree still grew inside.

Rebels
with a
Cause

SNUGGIES

My daughter gave me a set of long underwear for Christmas. They were on my list. Inge also gave me a gorgeous swanky pen in a leather box for book-signing, and a guidebook for Morocco (where we had been planning to travel). Inge has excellent taste, and these particular long undies are a beauteous shade of blue with a low-enough neckline not to show under clothes, a fuzzy interior to keep me warm, and a smooth silky exterior that feels luxurious.

So different from the so-called "flesh-colored" ones of my youth. I can vividly recall being driven to my first dance by a friend's mom who asked us sixth graders if we were wearing our Snuggies. She asked us in an excited tone that suggested that she was thrilled to share in our pre-pubescent adventure of going to our first dance and wearing nude-colored undies.

I did not own any Snuggies. Nor did my mother. She said she would rather freeze. My curiosity heightened, the next time my mother sent me to Kuszemba's Dry Goods Store to buy *pierogi* from the back window, I looked for signs of Snuggies. I passed counters stacked high with sheets, pillowcases, and towels, headscarves and aprons. No luck. I think you had to say a password to look at anything that began with the word "under."

The next time my mother took me shopping downtown at Marshall Field's, I begged to be taken to the Snuggies counter. My mother wondered why I was interested in these unattractive, horridly-colored clothes when she was willing to buy me almost anything else. An alpaca coat? A ruffly dress? She liked showing off to the neighborhood that our family was successful. I, on the other hand, wanted to blend in and be like the other kids. I asked for my hair to be cut like Buster Brown. She permed it to look like Shirley Temple. On the rare occasions when I took my lunch to school instead of walking home, I wanted it in a brown paper bag. She packed it up in a fancy lunchbox with frolicking flamingoes painted on the top.

Through Marshall Field's we strolled, past fur-collared jackets and cashmere sweater sets into the Intimates Department where counters featured pointy bras and lacy bridal lingerie. I was about to give up hope when I spotted them. Off in a corner, on a headless white mannequin, they were displayed in a Bermuda-shorts length bottom and undershirt-like top. My mother ran her fingers over the ribbed-knit cotton. Orangey-pink. She couldn't help but grimace. "Nude" was the idea. But like the Crayola flesh-colored crayon of that time, the color resembled no human's actual skin shade. I concluded that at the pre-teen dances where we girls stood in our socks on one side of the room and the boys on the other, we females were supposed to be wearing a pair of these practical, yet nude-suggestive items, to keep us both warm and safe from boys' curious hands wandering under our poodle skirts and sweater sets.

Searching the internet, I just learned that these days Snuggies are wearable plush blankets available in a wide variety of colors. They look cozy, perfect for cuddling up while watching TV. In the 1950s, Snuggies were quite a different item. Girls my age were acquiring their first bras and garter belts. If you wanted to look like Audrey Hepburn but stay warm and virginal in a Chicago winter, Snuggies were for you. Well, not so much for me. Although my mother conceded and bought me a pair, they stayed buried under my pajamas. I continued to wear pajama bottoms under my wool pants when ice skating or sledding.

Looking for Snuggies was part of my trying to unravel the mysteries of becoming a teenage girl in the '50s. Another mystery was why some of the girls started hanging out on street corners in small clusters, wearing identical clothes. Take my classmate Judy

Higgs, for example. She was someone we less hip kids would call "hoody." She wore the regulation hoody girl's wool jacket of charcoal gray with the collar turned up, revealing pink underneath. On her head she wore a babushka with the knot pulled up on her chin. All the other girls on the street corner were dressed exactly the same. Same jacket. Babushka knotted on the chin. Boys passed them and whistled. Sometimes they slinked over and issued complimentary insults. I didn't get it. Babushkas, really? Like their old country mothers wore, except pulled up on their chins? Gray wool jackets like boys wore but with pink under the collars instead of blue? Were they also wearing Snuggies under their tight skirts? I went over it again and again in my head to try to understand what they were doing and wondering if I should be doing it too.

The boys who strolled past and blew Lucky Strike cigarette smoke at these girls' lucky faces were usually Italian guys with D.A. haircuts from the next neighborhood. D.A. was short for duck's ass. High school boys with black wavy hair and enviable attitude. Through the second half of sixth grade and all of seventh, I watched these interactions and experienced a junior version of lust for these dark-haired smartass boys.

So different were they from Andrew Barnas, who often walked me home from school. Andrew was built like a snowman with a completely round head atop his completely round body. He usually spent our time together earnestly lecturing me about some topic particularly exciting to him. Greek mythology. Cytoplasm. Or there was Dennis Bara, who I knew practically from birth. Dennis walked me to school and called me his "Peachy Adorable." He lived across the alley in a basement apartment where the TV was constantly on. Dennis himself was a bland beige color and walked mostly on his tiptoes. He was as familiar and as boring as a saltine cracker.

And there was the boy I fell in love with in the 6th grade. Dickie Skwerski was in the 5th grade. Apparently, I always had a thing for younger men. Witness that my husband Tom is 10 years my junior. I met Dickie on the skating pond where I went daily after school. I watched Dickie play hockey while I tried to teach myself to twirl and jump. When Valentine's Day came around, I opened my piggy bank and went to Rudzinski's drugstore to buy the fanciest valentine I could buy. I always did have a flare for the dramatic. I gave it to Dickie. And he gave me one. Despite the fact that Dickie's valentine was of the variety one gave to every kid in your classroom, I was thrilled. It included a quarter with which Dickie was paying me back for a loan. I kept the valentine for years. He was that cute. And sweet. And nothing like the tempting Italian boys who pitched pennies in front of the candy store.

By 7th grade, Judy Higgs, with her made-up face and studied look of scorn, had the street-corner boys' full attention. But when she wasn't hanging out and flirting with Tony and Armando, she sought me out to be her friend. In the classroom cloakroom, she'd sidle up to me with some fake question like, "So didja do your homework, brainiac?" In class, she sat slouched and visibly bored, biting her fingernails to shreds, ink inexplicably staining her fingers. After school, she performed her part of the cool girls' ritual: babushka on chin, chewing gum, giving sidelong flirty yet aloof glances at the *Italiani*.

Many of the local neighborhood boys belonged to gangs. In our immediate vicinity, Polish boys belonged to the Drifters. My brother exhibited his naivete by actually asking our mother if he could join. She, of course, said no. My father put up a basketball net and boys with crewcuts came over to play.

The Italian boys with their matching jackets formed their own gang and I was fascinated. When I passed the arrogant boys pitching pennies and the girls pouting on the street corner, I felt a draw. Something about their rebellion, their operating outside the local authority, attracted me. But I wasn't sure I could pass the test to get in whatever society they had created. And if I did, would I really prefer chewing gum on the street corner wearing jeans that I had worn in the bathtub to get super tight to hearing Andrew Barnas spout about Hera and Clytemnestra?

By March, Judy Higgs started smiling at me when I walked by. Sometimes, she strolled away from her girl group to walk with me for a block. Did she want me as a friend, or did she want a way out of the street-corner group? Judy had become more familiar with her dyed and fried hair, her deep husky voice telling me, "I seen you at the dance last night. You looked kinda cute in that outfit. Next time let me give you a little lipstick, though, okay?" And the next time, I let her smear red on my lips, which I had to rub hard to remove before coming home.

In the late spring of 7th grade, it got warm enough for the hoody girls to shed their jackets and scarves. When we switched from long to short-sleeved white blouses for our spring uniform, I could see an inky blue shape on Judy's arm with some red swelling around it. Like the nosy nerd I was, I blurted out, "What happened to your arm?"

She explained the technique. "You're supposed to prick yourself a little with a razor, like makin' a shape with dots, y'know, and pour blue ink over it. Makes a kinda tattoo, get it? I got a little carried away with the cutting part, y'know?" I nearly fainted. "Doncha get yourself all worried on me. C'mon. Grow up!" My sensitive stomach did a flip. I didn't know anybody with a tattoo, homemade or not. Even my uncle in the Mafia didn't have one. And Judy's didn't look too sexy, neither.

My parents spent the spring putting the bakery up for sale and looking at new houses. That summer, we moved to the suburb of Niles. My mom packed up my training bras and garter belts and threw away my Snuggies. When September came, I started at my new school, St. John Brebeuf. Well-scrubbed 8th-grade girls with freckles and ponytails gathered at recess and invited me to play Red Rover. They stood in two lines facing each other, smiling. One side chanted, "Red Rover, Red Rover, let Marcia come over!" I ran to the other side, pushing through the line and laughing hard. Not a single babushka on a chin or self-inflicted tattoo.

I breathed a sigh of relief.

QUICK TO SPEAK

My Auntie Helene lived in a trailer park surrounded by freeways. Her unit was festooned with tiny white Christmas lights all year long. She had a couch and matching easy chair upholstered in a turquoise fabric that featured silvery threads, like bits of tinsel, running through.

Auntie Helene with Busia on a Florida vacation.

She hadn't always lived in a trailer. When I was a small child, she lived in an apartment with her husband Mike (christened Walter but called Mike, short for Mika, his last name, because we had too many Wallys) and their son, my cousin Wally. Their apartment was a treat for me to visit, with its movie magazines, colorful cosmetics, and bags of potato chips. A few blocks away, she worked in my family's bakery, where she was expert at tying up white cake boxes with string from the large spool that hung overhead. She was flawless at pushing loaves of bread through the slicer. But she was best at making quick and friendly banter with the customers in both English and Polish. She could talk faster, flirtier, and longer than any other human I've ever met. She later made good use of this skill when she became a switchboard operator.

Auntie Helene and me at a banquet in the church hall.

Auntie Helene always told me "Gawd never gave me a baby girl, but I don't mind because I have you." When I was 10, she gave me a diamond ring fancy enough for a wedding engagement. I'm ashamed to say that I left it on some soapy sink, in some unremembered restaurant bathroom. To the day she died, she told me how much she loved loved loved me.

For a short while, Auntie Helene tried living in a small suburban tract house with her second husband, Uncle Tommy. But Helene was more of a big-city girl. She wore her platinum hair in a tight perm. She slept with her eyebrows painted on. She liked her lipstick fire-engine red. When she was 60 and a 2-time widow, she dated a Black boyfriend who was 35. She liked getting people's attention.

———

I am the first college graduate in my family, but I attended three different colleges before I finished. The first was the University of Miami in Florida, a school my mother chose for me because it had the largest male-to-female ratio in the country, 14-to-1. She thought I was a little too bookish for my own good. Dutifully I went and dutifully I pledged the same sorority as the daughter of our neighborhood pharmacist, Mr. Rudzinski. Being a sorority girl sounded like a dream come true to my high-school-educated mother who spent her days carrying heavy pans of pumpernickel bread. I'm sure she pictured me dancing in ball gowns with tuxedo-wearing fraternity men. My life as she envisioned it gave her bragging rights in our immigrant factory neighborhood.

What she didn't know was that I had chosen a barefoot boyfriend who wore T-shirts with torn-off sleeves on which the words "SURFS UP" were writ large. A surfer poet. During a stormy hurricane warning, I sat on the beach cheering him on as he shot the curl on dangerous waters. I had met him while taking a philosophy course and he frequently recommended books for me to read. I lost my virginity to him one Easter morning. But when summer break came, he headed home to an old girlfriend in New Jersey. Devastated, I returned to Chicago.

So, when Gary the butcher asked me out, I accepted. I had seen him every day that summer at the Jewel Food Store where I had a temporary job as a cashier. Gary was blond and had an eager chubby face. I can't remember a single date with him except the one when he proposed. He took me to the Ivanhoe Restaurant, which had a medieval theme. There might have been singing waiters. On the dance floor, in the middle of a waltz, he pulled out a velvety box and popped the question. Despite the gnawing in my gut, I thought this was all terribly romantic and accepted the ring.

My mother was gravely disappointed. She had hoped I'd finish college and marry better than she had. She spent hours on the phone, sharing her feelings with anyone who'd listen. The family was abuzz and my elders were all advising me, "NO, don't do it!" All except Auntie Helene. She called me to say that she didn't know why people were so upset. She insisted that I was a smart girl and she trusted me. She said I would know what to do. I was in charge of my own life, after all.

Auntie Helene in her sixties.

What? I was responsible for my own decisions? I might determine my own future? I returned the ring. I returned to school. Christopher-Robin the surfer poet returned to me, and my "sisters" voted him Sorority Sweetheart. He proposed but I didn't marry him either. Neither did I stay long at University of Miami.

THE LAST PRESIDENT
OF EVERYTHING

My neighborhood friends, the kids I played hopscotch and kick-the-can with, wanted to start a club. Me too. We all desperately wanted to wear matching jackets like the older kids who belonged to gangs. The kids voted me in as president. We spent most of our meeting time trying to decide what style of jackets to get. My mom piled us all in her Buick and took us shopping. We settled on a striped summer jacket in shades of purple and blue. Okay, it was nothing like the tough jackets the gang kids wore. But we wore them rain or shine until the novelty wore off.

If our gang had a name, I don't remember it but I'm sure we spent a long, long time discussing what name to choose. After school let out, the temperatures soared into the 90s and low 100s and we switched to shorts and halter tops. We forgot what our purpose was, as if we ever had one. Our club did not live long. I was the first and last president.

When I was going into the 8th grade, my family moved to the suburb of Niles, Illinois, into a newly-built 3-bedroom brick ranch-style house with the fancy address of 7000 Jonquil Terrace. The neighborhood my mother chose was not completely devoid of familiar people. Our house was right down the street from Nora, one of my mother's Raindrops Club friends, and a few blocks from my Uncle Stash and Aunt Gerry. But there were also some welcome changes.

My new school was St. John Brebeuf, where the kids were of Polish, Italian, and Irish ancestry and all of the classes were in English. I felt great relief that there were no gangs on the streets, no corner taverns for fathers to get drunk in, no "hoody" kids.

It became clear that in order to fit in, I had to become a Girl Scout and earn badges in first aid and needlework. I came to know some of the other girls in my class over embroidery, as if it were the 18th century. After what seemed like forever, I was invited to join a club. A club! It was called The Triple F but the secret of what that meant would not be revealed to me until I was a full-fledged member. My imagination ran wild. I couldn't wait for the day of revelation.

When it was my turn to have the meeting at my new house, with its Floridian murals in the living room, my mom and I baked chocolate-chip cookies, and I was allowed to serve 7UP. Big smiles were on the other girls' faces when they revealed the meaning behind FFF. It stood for (*drumroll please!*) Funds for Flanigan. The purpose of the organization was to raise money for Father Flanigan, the pastor of our church. My heart fell. What? A fundraising group for the church? A club named for the overweight, acne-scarred, unattractive Irish parish pastor? At that moment, I longed to be back in the old inner-city neighborhood with the handsome and warm Father Mitch and the kids hanging out on the street corner, smoking cigs. Nonetheless, desperately wanting to be friends with somebody, anybody, I smiled widely and joined in on the plans for an upcoming bake sale. "You can make some of these delicious chocolate chip cookies!"

I was not shy about sharing my own fundraising and jacket-wearing ideas. Very quickly I rose up in the food chain and was elected President of the Triple F. I loved the honor of it. But alas, eventually I stopped calling meetings and the club fell apart. Miraculously, I remained friends with the girls, even through high school. Maybe they were all ready to move on to something else. And we did. FFF members started hosting dance and make-out parties in their finished basements. With boys!

When it came time for me to go to college, I headed to Miami, Florida, my mother's dream place to live. No winter! Palm trees! Year-round beaches! At the University of Miami, my assigned roommate, who put matching lavender bedspreads on our beds and re-arranged my books in order of color and size, insisted I go out for Sorority Rush. She was a Tri-Delt legacy, and they welcomed her with open arms. For the first couple of rounds, I imitated my roommate's wardrobe of Villager-brand skirts and blouses and maintained a somewhat subdued manner. Then, I warmed up to it and started talking more loudly, gesturing more broadly, telling family stories. I was, as the saying goes, being myself. I boldly wore a turquoise knit suit with matching patent leather go-go boots to the Alpha Chi house and was not invited back. I had worn uniforms while attending Catholic schools for 13 years and had little sense of sorority style. Several other houses also spurned me when I blasted in, gesticulating broadly and wearing too bright clothing for the sororal system. I quit formal Rush.

When informal Rush began, a few sororities on the lower end of the snob spectrum courted me. One of them included Mr. Rudzinski's daughter, Joyce. The Sigma Kappa sisters were varied in size, shape, hairstyle, and didn't mind my large personality. They asked me to join. When I told my mother, she was so excited, I felt I had to do it. Not having had the privilege of going to college herself, my mother was living through me during my first semester.

At the end of my sophomore year, you guessed it, I was prematurely elected president. I spent that summer attending the *Universidad de las Americas* in Mexico City, where I caught hepatitis eating octopus stewed in its own ink at some dive. At the beginning of my third year, when I would have been officially reigning as sorority prez, I ended up back home in Niles, Illinois. After weeks recuperating, I spent the rest of the academic year working at a publishing company. I never returned to Sigma Kappa or the University of Miami. Despite my mother's objections that everyone would look down at me at one of those Eastern girls' schools, I applied to Barnard College on the suggestion of one of my Miami professors. I happily moved to New York City. Still fantasizing that her daughter would become the sorority girl she'd always dreamed of being, my mother sent me a check so that I could become a lifelong member of Sigma Kappa. I used the money for a subscription to a Carnegie Hall concert series. Or maybe I just spent it on pizza and beer.

Decades later, I was the first and last Artistic Director of the Paper Moon Theatre Company.

You don't want to make me the president of anything.

LITTLE FART

My Busia (maternal grandmother extraordinaire) occasionally told us kids a story that made her blush and us guffaw. We begged her to tell the story of Fartchik over and over again because, let's face it, what eight-year-old kid doesn't find the word "fart" hilarious. Busia called the story "Fartchik," half-translating the original title into a Polish version of "Little Fart."

FARTCHIK (LITTLE FART)

A long time ago, there was a couple who wanted to have a child but could not. They tried for many years, asked everyone they knew for advice, and even got down on their knees and prayed for a baby. At last, when they were already getting up in years, an old midwife from another village took pity on them. She advised them to take a barrel, tie a piece of cheesecloth over one end, and every time they had to fart, they should fart into the barrel. It took three years, but eventually, a little baby appeared in the barrel. They decided to name him "Fartchik" or "Little Fart."

The old couple took special care of their child, and he grew and grew. When Fartchik was old enough, they asked him what he wanted to be.

"A blacksmith," said Little Fart.

"Good idea!" they said. And so, they arranged for him to be apprenticed to the best blacksmith for miles around. They took him each day to the blacksmith on a wagon filled with pillows so that their precious Little Fart would stay safe and sound. Every day Fartchik sat on his pillows and watched the blacksmith work. Months passed and Fartchik was getting a little bored, so he told the old couple that he was ready to graduate as a blacksmith.

The old man and woman were very excited. They built a blacksmith shop in their yard and bought a large amount of iron for Fartchik to work with. They couldn't wait to see what their precious Little Fart would make. Fartchik announced that he was going to make a wagon.

"Oh, how wonderful!" said the old people and they watched and waited. Fartchik moved pieces of iron around and hit them with a hammer now and then. Smoke came out of the smithery chimney. But then, Little Fart announced, "There is not enough iron here to make a wagon. I will make for you, instead, a wheelbarrow."

"Oh, how useful!" said the old people as they imagined how handy a wheelbarrow would be. They could carry wood from the shed to the house. They could move dirt out to the vegetable garden. Again, Fartchik moved pieces of iron here and there. Again, he hammered this and that. Again, smoke came out of the smokestack. But then, he announced, "There's not enough iron for a wheelbarrow. I'll make for you, instead, a pair of pliers."

"Oh, good!" said the old people, even though they already had several pairs of pliers. They wanted their son to succeed, so they smiled and urged him onward. Again, Fartchik moved around pieces of iron, which were now smaller than before. Again, smoke came out of the smokestack. Little Fart announced, "There's not enough iron to make a pair of pliers. I'll make for you, instead, a needle."

"Oh!" said the old woman. The old man was quiet because he had fallen fast asleep by now. The old woman wanted to be proud of her son. She was sleepy but she sat straight in her chair, watching as her son turned over and over the small piece of iron that was left. A tiny wisp of smoke came up from the smokestack. "Bprrrrrrrrrtt" was the sound it made, like the sound of a little fart.

The End!

SHAKESPEARE'S NOT FOR YOU

My divorce was final, and I needed to make some money. I received the house in the arrangement and the mortgage bills were high. My paltry earnings as a playwright were not going to cover them. I began to substitute-teach at local schools, mostly at the middle- and high-school levels. Subs were easy targets for students who wanted to taunt, bully, and make light of their teacher-for-the-day. My own teen daughter gave me instructions on how to keep order in the classroom. "Send them to the office!" she bellowed, as if she were the Queen of Hearts in *Alice's Adventures in Wonderland.*

I walked into an English class of 11th graders who had been performing at a low achievement level. I expected spitballs, paper airplanes, and a frog on my chair. But the class was quiet except for some whispering among a few girls with high hair. I looked at the lesson plan for the day: a discussion of their reading of a genre novel written at a 6th-grade vocabulary level. I was a bit embarrassed to be calling on 16-year-olds to read paragraphs aloud and then asking them questions, like: Who is the main character? What does she want?

A young woman stood up suddenly with tears in her eyes. "Please," she said. "Please do something. We know we're supposed to be reading Shakespeare. We're juniors. We're supposed to be reading *Romeo and Juliet.* Why aren't we good enough to read *Romeo and Juliet?*" She sat down and dabbed at her eyes with a tissue. The class was silent. No one disagreed.

What could I do? I was a mere sub, there for only a day. I didn't exactly have a copy of the play in my handbag. "I'll see what I can do." I wrote a little note to the teacher about the request, and I hoped it made a difference. I wish I had done more.

Years later, when I was writing *Now Let Me Fly*, a play about the *Brown v. Board* decision, I wanted to compose a speech for a similarly-aged girl who stood up in front of her school assembly of Black students in Farmville, Virginia, encouraging them to walk out, to go on strike in protest against their inferior school. I read everything I could about the case, conducted phone interviews, and made a trip to Farmville so I could talk with her fellow students and teachers. The other strikers told me that, regrettably, there was no record of what Barbara Johns said. Her sister told me, "Marcia, you are just gonna have to make it up." Another of the interviewees praised the teachers and community models they had had as students, telling me that they were lucky to have had people in their young lives who told them that, despite their circumstances, they could fly.

I grabbed the metaphor and ran with it. I also recalled the girl in the classroom who had bravely stood up and asked for Shakespeare to be in her life. The Barbara Johns monologue was the first scene of the play I wrote. Part of the speech reads, "I'm not talking about my hunger for food. No, I'm hungry for those shiny books they have up at Farmville High. I want the page of the Constitution that is torn out of my social studies book. I want a chance at that *Romeo and Juliet* I've heard about but they tell me I'm not fit to read."

As I write this, a story in the news tells of a statue of Robert E. Lee being taken down in the United States Capitol and a new sculpture being erected of Barbara Johns, the girl from Farmville, Virginia who spoke up.

GEFILTE FISH

My Catholic grandmother Victoria Kozial called out "*Oy Vey!*" when something went wrong. She regularly made gefilte fish. Jewish characters peopled her stories. As a child, I loved to listen to her dramatic and animated storytelling. While telling a Polish version of the Cinderella tale, she would enact the loss of the glass slipper by kicking her shoe across the room. For the Polish tale of the monster Smok, she would grind her teeth and growl, terrorizing her enraptured listeners. But she also told Jewish stories with enough matchmakers and violinists to people another *Fiddler on the Roof.* As a curious grownup, I asked her what percentage of her hometown had been Jewish. I was thinking maybe 10 or 15 per cent. She thought about the question with some seriousness, then answered, "About... (long pause) 90 per cent."

She had grown up in the shtetl! Victoria Kozial had been part of a Catholic minority in a Jewish village. If that wasn't enough, her husband (my grandfather), who came from the same region of Poland, spoke fluent Yiddish. Okay, he might have learned it to make deals at the South Water Street Market where he bargained for the tomatoes and cucumbers he sold on his cart. He did, after all, learn to speak Greek there. Or had he learned Yiddish in his home village? I'll never know.

When I visited Poland for the second time, I went to a relative's home on Cemetery Street, just across from a Jewish graveyard. In my splintered Polish I asked my auntie about her Jewish neighbors. She answered that there had been a huge number of Jewish families in Dębica "before the war." Then, large numbers of these friends and neighbors were taken away. During the German occupation, she hid a Jewish neighbor in her home. She had been pregnant at the time. She gave birth in the barn behind the house, not uttering a single sound so as not to attract attention to the hiding place in the house. I've read that Poles sometimes told such stories to take the blame off themselves for the atrocities of World War II. Yet I believed her. Since then, I've learned that organized Polish resistance to the Nazis was very strong in Dębica. Nevertheless, most of the Jews in the area were killed on the spot or taken to Auschwitz.

On the same trip, I visited Auschwitz. I walked through the horrifying gates and saw the exhibits that told the story more eloquently than words ever could: the piles of suitcases and shoes, the heaps of eyeglasses. Along the hallways were photographs of individual women and men clothed in the regulation black and white stripes that identified prisoners. I walked through these corridors where rows upon rows of faces looked straight forward. Emaciated, helpless. Silently, I read their names. And then, I saw a photo of a woman with my name. The Polish version of my name: Marysia Cebulska.

When writing *Visions of Right* in response to the anti-Jewish, anti-gay picketing ministry of the Westboro Baptist Church, I called upon my memories of trips to Poland. The Rev. Fred Phelps, the leader of the church at the time, responded to the play by calling me a "Jew-loving, fag-enabling whore of Babylon." I would love to have that on a T-shirt.

Escape &
Other Entertainments

Mom, Dad, Auntie Helene, & Uncle Mike Having Fun Long Before I Was Born

FLORIDA

My mother laughed as a parrot pulled the bobby pins out of her hair. The exotic birds were lined up on her outstretched arms before a backdrop of swaying palms. At home, there was winter and school, but we were vacationing in Florida.

My mother loved Florida. For several winters, she asked permission to take me and my brother Rich out of school, packed up a month's worth of worksheets and reading material, and headed south. Sometimes it was Mom and Dad and both of us kids on the car trip from Chicago to Florida. Often my grandparents accompanied us. One year my aunts and three girl cousins joined my mom and me for an all-female trip. Every time we passed a truck driver with dark hair, Aunt Dolores would sigh, missing her handsome husband who drove a milk route in rural Illinois. But mostly we teased and giggled. This was before the era of seat belts and my youngest cousin Louise stood up just behind the front seat for most of the trip. She jokes to this day about how she had "walked to Florida." We always stayed in cottages, purportedly so that some of our meals could be cooked in, lowering the cost of traveling to Paradise. But mostly it was so we could all be together. We visited alligator ranches and ate fish. We bought sundresses and new swimsuits and lazed around on beaches. We went to Parrot Jungle.

Decades later, I wrote a play called *Florida*. Theatre producers from the Sunshine State called me for copies of the script. I had to disappoint them with a play about an abused wife living in Chicago, only dreaming of an escape to Florida.

Female family members on a winter trip to Florida: my Aunt Dolores, Mom, Busia, me, my cousins Susan, Dorina, and Louise. We all traveled together in one sedan.

SMOK

In the main square of Krakow, a man dressed as Smok,
taking a break from wearing his mask.

My grandmother spoke in her heavily-accented voice, "I don't have to tell you it was long time ago, because you know it was long time ago, back when Poland was very young." We kids stopped hitting each other with pillows and braiding each other's hair. The six of us gathered our pajamaed selves around on the tousled beds, vying for positions closest to Busia's knees. We were in for a treat. We had begged her repeatedly to tell us a story and she had put us off, pleading tiredness. But now, well past our bedtime, she started to tell us the familiar tale. She continued, "There was a great big monster called SMOK!" Her eyes widened. Our eyes widened. We delighted in being scared.

"Smok ate up people's goats and sheep, then their pigs and cows." She raised her volume, "Soon, they were afraid he was going to eat people!!!!" We clenched our teeth in fear that Smok might come and gobble us up. Never mind that we were in my aunt and uncle's farmhouse, 4,700 miles from the monster's lair.

Busia leaned back as if to take a moment's breath. "The people didn't know what to do so they went to Krak, the wise man of the village. He calmly nodded his head and told them to come back in the morning." My grandmother always added a wisdom-conveying aside at this point, "Because you should always think first." She pointed to her head at this point, the location, after all, of her thinking and said, "And Krak thought with 'dish,'" meaning "this." She laughed at her own playful self-mockery of her immigrant pronunciation. We were relieved by the moment of levity. But not for long.

"In the morning, Krak told the people of the village to cut open the belly of a cow and fill it with sulphur, what they make matches from. Then they should throw the cow into the 'yama,' the great big 'yama,' of the monster." We understood this to be a cave. "The people, they watched and waited."

At this point, Busia would point to my brother and my older boy cousin Wally and say, "Some teenage boys, like Porkush and Ritchie here, climbed up a tree so they could see what Smok was doing. And the people asked them, 'What is he doing now?'

"And the boys answered, 'He's eating the legs!'

"What is he doing now?" Busia intensified the volume, nudging our own teen boys.

"He's eating the head!" answered my brother and Wally.

"What is he doing NOW!!!?"

"He's eating the belly!!! We kids were all on the edge of our beds, chewing the ends of our blankets.

Busia lowered to a whisper, "What is he doing now? He's drinking from the stream."

"There was," she explained, "a big stream that ran through the yama, the great big yama. The sulphur burned him inside and made him thirsty. So, what is he doing now?"

The boys said, "He's drinking and drinking!"

"And what's happening to him?"

"He's getting bigger and bigger."

And Busia took over with her most dramatic voice, "And bigger! And bigger! And he got so BIG, he BUST!" We all exhaled with relief, as if Smok's cave had been next door.

"And then the people, they carried dirt, lots of dirt, and buried Smok in his cave and heaped even more dirt on top until there was a great big hill. And the people were so happy, they went to Krak, the wise man, and made him king of Poland. The first king of Poland. And they named the town after him. Krakow."

At last, the monster vanquished, and order restored, we children could sleep in peace.

———

Many years later, my daughter and I stood on the Krakow cathedral steps beneath a huge tusk. What looked like a mastodon tooth was labeled "Smok's Tooth." My cousin Bruno pretend-growled with a smile and warned, "Smok is coming!!!" All around us, children, street performers, and playful dads dressed as dragons were also warning, "Smok is coming!!!" On a family heritage trip with Inge, we just happened to visit the old capital during Smok Days. We stood on the hill that the people had made in this lovely city named after, not a general or a swordfighter, but a wise man who stayed home and, when asked, gave thoughtful advice.

Me, pointing up at "Smok's Tooth" with Inge looking up.

A child wearing part of a Smok costume.

Delighted, we took tours of Smok's cave and the castle. Parades and processions led by dragons greeted us on the square. Funny, but I had never thought of Smok as a dragon. And you, probably, have never even heard of this giant rampaging creature.

A tape I had made as a folklore graduate student recording my grandmother's telling of the Smok story came in handy during a production of my play *Florida*. My friend and theatre collaborator Martha Jacobs listened repeatedly to it. She wanted to get just the right regional accent for the lead role. Martha took apart the language into phonetic syllables and reassembled the play with the exact regional pronunciation of my immigrant grandmother. Her painstaking work paid off in a breathtaking performance.

THE OAT FIELD

My cousin Susan married a pig farmer. She grew up on a farm, and I often spent time visiting her during summer vacations when we were kids. Our mothers were sisters and close. One steamy day, Susan and I tunneled our way through a field of oats across from the farmhouse. We flattened a small area in the middle of the field, so we couldn't be seen from the road. Every day we carried out a toy or two to our secret place. Every day, we flattened out a larger area where we played checkers and dressed our dolls in tiny bathing suits and wedding dresses as flies buzzed overhead. We continued to flatten the oats, claiming more and more territory, adding more and more toys. No one told us that the giant machine was going to come, a huge green harvester with yellow lettering. When we heard the monster groan, we ran to the barn and pretended to concentrate on scraping the floor clean of manure.

At suppertime, my uncle's face was burning red. Like most of the men in our family, his name was Walter. My father, three uncles, and one cousin were all named Walter. We called this one Uncle Wally or by his last name, Dravis. He was suntanned, broad-shouldered, tall, and dressed in overalls, unlike my own Chicagoan father, who was more dapper and citified. That evening Uncle Wally was biting his lower lip. After he showered in the basement, he took my Aunt Dolores to the baby-changing room off the kitchen and talked with her in an insistent, impatient tone. Then, he sat down at the table and lifted an eager, hungry toddler onto his lap. Over dozens of visits, I never saw a highchair in that home with six children.

On the farm, we had our big meals at lunch—platters of baked chicken or braised beef, garden vegetables in abundance, bowls of ice cream with peaches. At suppertime, we ate small, quick, easy-to-prepare meals. Aunt Dolores came to the table to serve up some reheated jarred tamales. After grace, I shifted bits of the yellow and brown food aimlessly around my plate.

Once the table was cleared, Aunt Dolores looked us in the eye and told us that we had done a bad thing. Not only did we ruin half the oat crop with our trampling, but expensive machinery had been halted when it tried to consume our dolls and toy trucks. Her voice was even and calm. We hung our heads low. We didn't complain about our beheaded mangled dolls.

My cousin Susan swore she would never marry a farmer. Yet here she is, married to a pig farmer. Her first husband had been a city man who had wooed her with diamonds and pearls and later wanted to be paid back. Her second marriage is to a kind man she's known since high school. At family get-togethers, Susan reminds me of our oat field-flattening escapade as her man Bill plays the guitar and sings.

My cousin Susan at Parrot Jungle, far away from the farm.

THE DEVIL AND
THE TAILOR

My grandmother draped a measuring tape around my neck and smiled. "There," she said, "now, you are a tailor."

I immediately felt like a star, proud of myself, even though I hadn't sewn a single stitch. I had wanted to earn a needlework badge in girl scouts, but I didn't know a single thing about sewing. I suspect the idea behind never teaching me was that, if I never learned, I wouldn't end up in a sweatshop, like my dear Busia had in her youth. But here I was, wanting to learn so that I could be like the other 8th grade girls at my new suburban school, maybe even be a step ahead.

Busia continued her lesson by telling me a story. No surprise. Busia did all her teaching with folktales, stories, and jokes. Now, to help me learn to sew, she would tell me the story of The Devil and the Tailor.

"The devil, he challenged the tailor to a contest. Who could sew the hem onto a cape the fastest?" Busia smiled with glee at the idea of this competition. "First, they had to thread their needles. The devil chose the biggest needle with the biggest eye to make his job easy." I looked over at my grandmother's pincushion loaded with needles and saw the immediate appeal of a big needle. I picked one up. "But the thread, it kept coming out, and the devil, he had to keep threading and re-threading. The tailor chose a small needle so he could make fast, small stitches." I put the big needle back and picked a smaller one. Busia dampened the end of a short length of thread in her mouth and put the thread through the eye of the needle. She tied a knot at the end.

"The devil made huge, loose stitches, trying to get more done faster, but without a knot, his stitches kept coming out. The tailor made small, even stitches, like this." Her hand moved with a rapid rhythm. "The tailor sewed quickly and beautifully, and he won. He kept his soul and got a nice cape in the bargain." I imitated my Busia's movements, albeit clumsily, and reluctantly learned about the downside of taking a short cut.

THE POLKA KING

Aunt Virgie & Uncle Wally on their wedding day,
with my grandfather and grandmother.

My Uncle Wally Kozial (yes, another Walter!) and his wife
Virgie were the Polka King and Queen of the World. Uh-
huh. World polka-dancing champions. They had danced
all their married life, but once their six children were grown, they
traveled the planet dancing in competitions. And winning. For those
who are in the dark about such things, dancing a polka is something
like doing a very fast waltz. One-two-three. One-two-three. Uncle
Wally specialized in doing a double-time polka that he learned from
his immigrant father, my grandfather Stanley. On the rare occasions

that I was asked to dance with either of them, I could hardly keep up.

Wally was my godfather. He was also the golden boy of the family. Super smart, he was the only one of the six children to log some college credits. Super brave, he was a tail gunner and fighter pilot during WWII. And, yes, that's probably what got him into Syracuse University, using the G.I. Bill of Rights. Super clever, he gave up his wholesale fruit and vegetable route to successfully play the stock market.

My godfather Wally, a pilot during World War II.

My mother would say of her brother, "We call him 'Midas' because everything he touches turns to gold." I probably owe him my own college degree since my mother paid for my tuition from profits on the stock exchange, where she invested under Uncle Wally's tutelage. Note that I might have earned a scholarship given my excellent scoring on the National Merit scholarship exams, but my mother did not want me to carry the scourge of being a "scholarship student." Go figure.

King Midas suffered dire consequences from turning everything to gold, and so did Uncle Wally. Who knows when or why, but a giant rift developed in the family, with Wally and his wife on the other side of the fence from everyone else. For decades, my cousins and I have been trying to figure out what happened and why.

Like my other aunties, Virgie worked in my parents' bakery, in close proximity to my mother. The story goes that she accused my mom of having an affair with her husband. "With my own brother!" my mother would exclaim loudly. I was too young to understand what an affair or incest meant, but whatever it was, my mental response was, "Whatever it is, how would mom have the time?" My mother supervised the store, kept the books like a whiz accountant, and was president of several church and school organizations, as well as being a mom of two. She cleaned the house, cooked for the bakers, and had her phone flirtation with Father Mitch to keep her busy. Was this accusation the source of the rift?

My cousin Louise has suggested (note that in our 60s and 70s, we are still talking about this) that it was a class matter. She posits that the senior members of our family may have looked down on Auntie Virgie's family. Something about the area where they came from in Poland. I wondered: How could you get any poorer than people who possessed only two bowls to eat from? Folks who only had one? Although I did hear my beloved grandmother refer to some people as from the "other side of the tracks," it usually was an insult she hurled based on rude behavior, not financial status. But maybe there was something to it and I just don't like to think of my family as snobbish.

The explanation that most clicked for me was an account of an unexpected visit from my grandmother to her son and daughter-in-law's home. Wally and Virg had moved up from the old neighborhood in the city to a sprawling ranch style house in the suburbs. One day, Busia knocked on the door unexpectedly and Virgie peeked out between the drapes to see who it was. Virgie told the kids to go to their rooms and be quiet. Having seen Virgie peeking through the curtains, Busia knocked again. Virgie turned the lights out. Busia got into her Buick and drove off in a huff. This was not Polish hospitality. She felt spurned.

Meanwhile, Virgie hung her head in shame. She just couldn't have let her mother-in-law see the house in its disastrous state. Babies were running around in dirty diapers; toddlers screamed with jam-smeared faces; furniture was tipped over by rowdy boys; there were scrawls on the wall in stolen lipstick. (Or at least that's the way the story goes. We weren't there.) Maybe Busia should have called in advance. Maybe Virgie should have answered the door a crack and told her to please come back another time. They both felt guilty. They both felt wronged. No one was going to apologize. The incident reminded each of them of earlier slights. The rift grew. Wally sought counsel from the parish priest (nobody in that generation of our family ever went to a therapist) who told him that his allegiance had to be with his wife. Cleaving and all that. Wally and Virgie took their polka dancing to the next level.

A decade or so later, Virgie read some advice books about mending fences in broken families. She took the message to heart. She apologized humbly to my Busia, who accepted. And, thankfully, both sides could attend family gatherings once again. Wally and Virg attended my first wedding and my daughter's christening. They stuffed cash into my hands at every visit. Virgie smiled broadly.

When my Aunt Dolores died, Wally and Virg, then 80, came to the funeral. At the funeral lunch, Tom and I sat at a table with my cousin Wally and his wife and Uncle Wally and Virg. Virg told a story of how she once felt like she needed to spice up her marriage. Things had gotten cool between her and Wally. She had so much to do with the kids and the big house to clean. Virgie went to the priest (maybe even the same one) and asked him what to do. He gave her instructions, and she followed them to a tee. She made a date with Wally to go to the movies. She wore the fancy full-length mink coat he had bought for her with some of their first stock-market earnings. In the movie theatre, as Cary Grant was putting his arm around Doris Day, Wally put his arm around Virgie. Wally ran his hand over the luxurious fur and onto his wife's neck. Something was different. He ran his hand down under the collar of the coat, down her back, and then opened the front just a teensy tad. Virginia Kozial, his wife and the mother of his children, was entirely naked under the mink coat.

Yes, my 80-year-old Aunt Virgie was telling this story to us younger couples. We found ourselves mildly amused and a lot embarrassed. We laughed nervously but Virg and Wally were sitting there, holding hands. They added details of how they had recently won another international polka-dancing competition.

In 1997, Wally and Virgie attended my second wedding, which we celebrated with several musical groups and theatrical performances. My elderly aunt and uncle had made the five-hour car trip from Chicago. At the reception, while a band called the Dancing Elephants played, my Uncle Wally addressed me quietly, "Do you think they could play a polka?"

A Family That Prays Together, Stays Together

NUN DOLLS

My cousin Wally collects nun dolls. Twenty or so of them are lined up on a shelf that surrounds the front hall so that, as you climb the stairs, you are surrounded by miniature nuns. All stand with perfect posture in pristine boxes, facing out through cellophane windows, outfitted in their traditional habits complete with veils and rosaries. Franciscans, Dominicans, Felicians, Sisters of Charity.

Wally always liked nuns. For decades, he's kept in touch with the Franciscans of the Blessed Kunegunda who taught us in grade school, back when he was still nicknamed "Porky." Now, most of them have passed on or are living out their last years at the motherhouse in Lemont, Illinois. Sister Angeline, Sister Dolorine, Hedwig, Edwina. Every year, Wally visits them. His wife Carol is more than happy to join him.

In their younger days, Wally and Carol had both been in the religious life. Carol had been part of the Franciscans of the Sacred Heart community. But her life changed, and she became a dental hygienist in a gleaming white uniform instead. She met Wally while cleaning his teeth.

Walter Valentine Mika had once aspired to be a priest. Later, he entered a monastery. Wally once jokingly blamed me for his being asked to leave the monkhood. He said that on a particular Visitation Day, after the Solemn High Mass, I ran toward him and publicly bestowed a plentitude of hugs and kisses on his tall self. The way he tells the story, the senior brothers frowned on "that blonde" embracing him. They suspected he wasn't serious about his vow of celibacy.

It couldn't have been me. Not that I didn't have blonde hair or hadn't given him a hug or two. In our teens, Wally and I were close. It's just that I know I would have been more restrained that day, seeing as how I was on the arm of his best friend Bob, who I was dating at the time. I held Bob's hand and leaned my head on his shoulder at every opportunity.

In my memory, it was Wally's platinum-haired mother who clasped him in an enthusiastic embrace on that fateful visiting day. My Aunt Helene had once been a girl singer in a Big Band in Chicago, wearing spangly evening dresses and bright red lipstick, singing in a sultry alto voice. As in the movies, she had fallen in mad, passionate love with the trumpet player. As Wally recently put it, he had attended his own parents' wedding.

Aunt Helene gave the longest, tightest, and most enthusiastic hugs on the planet. On that Visitation Day, wearing a jaunty hat and her fur stole, with its mink mouths fashioned as clasps biting other minks' tails, she ran toward her son, called out his nickname, threw her arms around him, and lifted her high-heeled shoes off the ground. Still clad in ecclesiastical robes, Wally held her in mid-air, joy on his face. He was thrilled his mom was there, had witnessed him in procession with the other monks-in-training. He was delighted.

It's too bad the senior monks didn't allow him to stay. His gorgeous tenor voice would have been superb chanting Gregorian in a monkly choir. Instead, he made use of it in the Chicago opera company he joined. And the monks could have used the caring qualities that he displayed when he later became a nurse. Fortunately, they came in handy when he went to work with AIDS patients in Africa. He also joined the army and kept being promoted until he made colonel. He always liked a good uniform.

Wally and Carol married and raised four children. They lived in Germany for a few years and to this day enjoy taking trips to Europe, staying in convents and monasteries. I visited them recently in San Antonio, where they live in a large brick house with palm trees outside and plenty of room inside to display their collections of rolling pins and nun dolls.

My cousin Wally's wedding to Carol, with Bob as best man.

SUNSTROKE

At a wedding reception: my mom, paternal grandmother,
Uncle Hank, my dad, and Aunt Olga.

My father's family members were taller, thinner, quieter, and more distant than my maternal relatives, who lived at a high volume and could be crushingly affectionate and rowdy. When, as a young person, I asked Mom where my father's people, the Cebulskis, came from, she said from the Eastern side of Poland, close to Russia. Her own family clustered between Krakow and the Tatra mountains. It was the 1950s, era of the Cold War, and Dad's origins came off to me as forbidding.

My father's father had died when Dad was only a child, reportedly of a sunstroke. Since I had been hospitalized myself for a feverish overexposure to the sun, I believed the account. When I was in my 40s, my psychotherapist told me that "sunstroke" could have been code for overindulgence in alcohol.

We rarely visited my dad's family, or them, us. Except, that is, for my father's brother, Uncle Hank. My mom told me that once upon a time, before he married Aunt Olga, he lived with my mom and dad in their pre-bakery house on Luna Street. People would ask her which one was her husband and which one was the boarder. She always blushed after she said that and, as a child, I wasn't quite sure why. Even now I am only guessing that it maybe had something to do with an intimation of intimacy, as if she had been living in a threesome. My Uncle Hank did have dark wavy hair which, at the time, was considered a desirable feature. And he was always dressed up in pressed, fine-tailored suits and swanky ties. When I was nine years old, I didn't get it. I considered my farm uncle, Wally Dravis, in his overalls, and the parish priest, Father Mitch, in his white collar, far more handsome.

Eventually, Uncle Hank married Aunt Olga and they had a son. Gregory was probably (okay likely) a fine, regular kid, but my brother and I decided from the day of his birth to hate him. We told him he was spoiled since he was an only child. We refused to share our toys with him and called him bratty. Maybe it was because we didn't care for his mother so much. She smiled a lot, but I never thought her grins were genuine. She wore padded shoulders and had her hair coiled and sprayed hard. But the worst thing was that she would take me aside and tell me nasty tales about my grandmother, my mom's mom, who lived with us. Olga would confide in me as if I were a grownup that she thought it was my grandmother's fault that my father and mother didn't get along. All my grandmother's fault. My beloved grandmother, the person who cut up ripe, juicy peaches for me to eat when I was hot and sweaty from playing. My grandmother, who sewed matching clothes for my dolls. Because of Olga, I developed a sense of distrust about that branch of the family and took it out on Gregory.

My father's youngest brother was an occasional visitor, too. He was tall, thin, and blondish, like my brother. My mother was matron of honor at his wedding, and she looked gorgeous in the photos. People often said my mom looked like Elizabeth Taylor. I wouldn't go that far, but she was an ethnic beauty, with blue eyes and dark hair and an almost ever-present infectious smile. I say "almost" because she could become quite angry when we didn't do our chores. I have a distinct memory of her threatening my brother with a vacuum cleaner hose. We did test her patience.

When sorting through the family photos, I ran across some from that that wedding party. Although I can't even recall my uncle's name, when I saw a photo of him, I let out an involuntary, "No!" Memories flashed across the screen of my mind from my father's days as a gambler and thief.

THE GAMBLER

*My father and his dog Beans on the back porch of our
first home on Luna Street.*

My Daddy was a gambling man. He shot craps, bet on the ponies, and played high-stakes poker. He was also the president of the Holy Name Society at St. Stanislaus, Bishop & Martyr Catholic Church; a baker of such high repute that customers lined up outside our family bakery well before the doors opened; and a cake decorator of such artistry that Northwestern University asked him to teach the craft, despite his limited sixth-grade education. He was a husband, a barfly, and a father of two. But it was the gambling that led to the fraud that led to the federal case that led to the national newspaper attention he earned as a hoaxer, a liar, and a thief.

It was 1949 and I was a kindergartener. My mother had tucked me into bed before leaving to conduct a meeting as president of St. Stan's Mother's Club. When thunking sounds awakened me, I padded my way in my footed jammies across the gray linoleum floor to the living room. There, my father and his youngest brother were tossing encyclopedia volumes onto the floor. The safe was hidden behind the heavy books, even I knew that. It was a family joke that the $22,000 in savings bonds intended to pay for us kids' college education was hidden behind *The Book of Knowledge* (wink-wink). In 1940, the median home price in the U.S. was under $3,000, making $22,000 a considerable sum.

A young couple with two small children, my parents took a risk going into business, but they worked hard and saved the money over a five-year period. The bakery was open from 6:30 a.m. to 6:30 p.m. Tuesday through Saturday and till noon on Sundays. Most nights, bakers were busy mixing dough, baking rye and pumpernickel breads, babkas, and kolaczki. In our bilingual neighborhood, most customers spoke and ate Polish.

On Friday nights, my brother and I gobbled up rye bread straight out of the brick oven. We spread copious amounts of butter onto the warm slices flecked with caraway seeds. On holidays, local women came to my father, carrying their turkeys and hams for him to roast, since most of the kitchens in our blue-collar neighborhood lacked ovens. He would set a fire inside the oven, and once the bricks were heated, sweep out the ashes. He then pushed huge paddles into the mouth of the oven, carrying cake pans or bread dough, turkeys or hams. It was hot, demanding work.

On Mondays, when the store was closed, my father often went to the racetrack. My mother urged him to take up golf with the neighborhood physician, Dr. Stryz, but my father believed he worked hard and deserved his own kind of treat. And who knows? He might get lucky. Daddy came home on luckier days handing out $2 bills for us kids, which we received with glee and confusion. My brother Rich and I had a racetrack boardgame and knew the names of famous racehorses like Seabiscuit. But the $2 bills seemed a little fake to us, and we were always surprised when we could use them to buy Lik-m-aids and Tootsie Rolls at Serafin's grocery store across the street.

On the days Daddy didn't do so well, he went to a tavern to console himself. Sometimes, on such afternoons, the police would telephone Mommy to tell her that Daddy had smashed up the car against a tree or a brick wall. Our parents always replaced the totaled vehicle with the latest model of a Buick Roadmaster. My parents, after all, had a reputation as community leaders to uphold. When my father lost at the track, he sometimes hit my mom. My mother would buy herself another Anne Fogarty dress to soothe her feelings. Despite the fact that the exterior of our house was covered in tar paper, my mother wore Shalimar perfume and had a collection of leather coats in different colors, including persimmon. As a little girl, I loved to say the word "persimmon," but it took me 14 years before I tasted one. I liked trying on my mom's clothes and dousing myself in her fragrance.

But on that night, I was standing in my jammies, puzzling over what I beheld. My father turned around and noticed me peeking from behind the Florida-themed screen that separated the living room from my parent's bedroom. I decided it was time to speak. "What are you doing, Daddy?" I tried to tell myself he was working on some fatherly do-it-yourself project like making the bookshelves bigger, but my heart was thumping wildly in protest.

"Go back to bed, Honey. Go back to bed. Your mommy is gonna be upset if you're walking around at night." It's true that I worried my mother with my vivid dreams and sleepwalking.

Dutifully, I went back to bed, but I kept on hearing the encyclopedia volumes hitting the floor and the whispers of the grown men. Although I was accustomed to the bakery help walking through the house to use the bathroom or the phone or to eat some of my mother's famous soups, I knew this was different. I wished my brother's bedroom wasn't so far away. I wondered if he heard the unfamiliar sounds. Probably not. He slept like a log. I tried to listen instead to the rhythm of the giant mixers in the bakery shop that shared a wall with my small bedroom. I tried to picture my father back where he should be, among the bakers in his white T-shirt, pants, and flour-covered shoes, mixing the sours for the rye bread, frosting cakes, or slicing strawberries.

In the morning, the grownups were upset. Somebody had tampered with the front door lock. Somebody had shelved the encyclopedia volumes in the wrong order. Somebody had stolen the bonds. I tried to attract my mother's attention to tell her what I'd seen, but all she could say was, "Not now!" My Auntie Helene whisked me away to school.

Sister Mary Crescentine was trying to rehearse us in the alphabet song, but I wasn't listening. I was thinking hard to recall everything I knew about my father. I knew that as a 10-year-old, Wally Cebulski had apprenticed as a baker, forced to leave the sixth grade to support his mother and siblings after his father's death. I felt sorry for him because I loved school and wanted to be a teacher. I wondered what he'd have become if he had gone to high school. Fortunately, I reminded myself, he had become an expert at cake decoration. With waves of icing and a flick of his wrist, he created wedding bells, swans, and bridal dresses. His elaborate, tiered cakes earned us invitations to wedding celebrations almost weekly. We went as a family to upstairs halls for receptions where we helped ourselves from giant platters of food and danced to live polka bands.

A few days later, I told my mother what I thought I'd seen my daddy do, but she dismissed it instantly as a bad dream. I was not to talk about these adult matters. My daddy was a good man, a generous man. Hadn't he given a $1,000 chalice to our church? Maybe she was right. Maybe I had been dreaming. Maybe I had been sleepwalking. My father reported the theft, applying for a replacement of the stolen bonds.

The federal inquiry investigated the bank where the bonds had been cashed and compared my father's signature to the endorsements. They brought in a lie-detector expert. They empaneled a grand jury and called in the Secret Service to question possible suspects.

During the 18-month investigation into the theft of the bonds, my father tried hard to be an ideal family member. According to the social pages of the *Marengo Republican-News*, he created a special cake for my cousin Louise's christening:

"The cake was 2 feet in diameter and centered with a doll wearing an off-the-shoulder gown of whipped cream, the skirt of her gown was formed by the cake covered with a whipped cream icing formed into white and pink roses and lacy edges and spangled with silver beads" (March 23, 1950).

Louise was his godchild. For her first birthday, my daddy outdid himself and created a carousel cake featuring moving confectionery animals that he himself had fashioned. My cousins and grandparents stood in wonder watching the sugar giraffes and bears move up and down while circling the cake top in a merry-go-round.

The merry-go-round stopped when the police took my father out of the house in handcuffs. Under questioning by Hardy D. Anheier, head of the Chicago office of the Secret Service, my father, Walter T. Cebulski, repeatedly denied his involvement in stealing the bonds but offered to drop the appeal for reimbursement. Under continued questioning, he stumbled, and finally confessed. He said he had gambled on the horses, hoping to get rich. When he lost it all, he was afraid to tell his wife.

Newspaper articles about the case appeared across the country. Headlines read:

**BAKER'S $22,000 LIE TO WIFE PUTS HIM
IN U.S. JAM**
(*Chicago Tribune* 7/10/51)

BONDS STOLEN—BY HORSES!
(*The Akron Beacon Journal* 7/10/51)

LIE DETECTOR EXPERT SOLVES MYSTERY
OF VANISHED BONDS
(*Kansas City Times* 7/10/51)

T-MEN FIND SLOW HORSES, NOT THIEVES,
GOT BONDS
(*Lebanon Daily News* 7/10/51)

CASHES BONDS TO PLAY HORSES,
SAYS THEY WERE STOLEN
(*Jacksonville Daily Journal* 7/27/51)

Mothers of my playmates stopped me on the street and asked if my father was going to prison. Others asked if we had plans to leave the neighborhood. At church, fellow parishioners looked at us with curiosity, or pity, or they avoided looking at us altogether.

Daddy fell to his knees and begged my mother's mercy. Mommy went to the pastor at St. Stan's to ask for advice. The priest told her to forgive, to take her husband back, to say it was all right that he had cashed the bonds and hadn't told her the truth. That she should turn the other cheek. The priest told her to attend the church carnival that night on her husband's arm, holding her head high, as if nothing had happened.

It was 1951. She did what she was told.

*Mom and Dad on a Mother's Day trip to a
flower show downtown.*

*My dad helps himself to food from a dish
held by my mom.*

One of my father's famous wedding cake creations.

THE CRUSH

*My mom as a harem girl, Father Mitch as a cowboy,
and Mom's friend Nora as another harem girl.*

My mother was in love with a priest. When she recognized his voice on the phone, ordering rye bread and raspberry donuts for the church rectory, her tone turned flirty. She had a special voice, just for him. My brother Rich and I teased her about it. But who could blame her? Father Mitch was strikingly handsome, with shiny black hair and a laugh that made everyone in the room join in. When you talked to Father Mitch, he listened as if you were the only person in the universe. He designed costumes for fundraising variety shows, and my mother performed in them. At one particular church masquerade party, he wore a fitted black cowboy shirt with a white kerchief around his neck. My mother dressed as a harem girl.

When my dad was working in the evenings, as he often was, Father Mitch would accompany my mom, my brother, and me on excursions. Sometimes we went to Riverview amusement park where we rode on roller coasters and ate cotton candy. So as not to scandalize anyone, he removed his collar, and we called him "Uncle Mitch." My brother and I adored him. Photos show us looking up at him with delight on our faces. I'm sure that while we kids rode the Tilt A Whirl, my mom was confiding her troubles to the neighborhood's best listener.

Left to right in back: Uncle Mike, Auntie Helene,
Sister Dolorine, cousin Wally, Father Ed.
In front: Father Mitch and me.

We rarely saw my father in a playful mood. Most days, Dad walked around, exhausted in a white undershirt, a stained apron, and flour-encrusted shoes. He was distant, disappeared on benders, and had fits of rage.

Unlike my father, my mother had attended high school. She wore designer clothes and took me for tea at Marshall Fields. She belonged to the Rosary Society and was founder and president of the Mother's Club. Mom loved to laugh and dance.

When I was a teenager, my recently-divorced mother told me some of the history of her marriage. She was only 18 at her wedding, and, after six months, she knew her marriage had been a mistake. Since the church forbade divorce, her parents encouraged her to give it more of a try. Things would be different when there were children. She gave birth to my brother Rich and then me. She and my dad made large contributions to the church and entertained other business owners. They became pillars of the community. He became more violent.

I do not know if Father Mitch and my mother held hands, much less kissed. I do know they stayed friends, remained in contact, and shared long phone calls till the end of their lives.

When my mother was in her fifties and I was a full-grown adult, she, my Aunt Helene, and I took a ride to the country to visit my Aunt Dolores. As was her wont, Helene sneakily passed me sticks of gum and chocolate mint meltaways, as she used to do in my childhood. We sang along with the radio, voices harmonizing. When a particularly long romantic song ended, Helene continued to rhythmically drum her fingers on the dashboard. She turned to my mom and said, "You and Mitch should have gotten married years ago." My mother replied with silence. I don't know if it was embarrassment or the welling up of tears that kept her quiet.

Father Mitch and me at a picnic on my grandparents' farm. He was always attentive, appropriate, and kind.
I adored him.

Fame
and
Shame

SHA SHA & CHI CHI

My brother Rich and baby me outside our
new home in the bakery.

My brother was named Richard, but I called him Chi Chi. When I was a toddler, I just couldn't get my mouth around the two Rs. In return, he called me Sha Sha. He was almost five years older than me, so I'm sure he could handle the pronunciation. He was just being playful, and I loved it. So we were Sha Sha and Chi Chi.

When I was about seven, we acquired our first television set, and I became familiar with Zsa Zsa Gabor. Longing for such dramatic style, I hoped everyone would call me Sha Sha forever. I believed it bestowed on me a glamorous air. I imitated the Gabor Hungarian accent and pretended to flaunt a long cigarette holder. As a budding adolescent, Chi Chi barely looked up from his board games to groan about what an actress I had become.

As Chi Chi and I grew, we became so different you'd think we'd been born on separate planets. He was fastidiously tidy. I was so messy, teachers sent notes home complaining about flies circling my desk. I adored school. My brother, on the other hand, only wanted to run bases and shoot hoops. He barely endured one year of college; I gleefully went to grad school. He decorated his house in a monochrome purity that included white wall-to-wall carpeting, a white baby grand, and a white dog. I gave new meaning to "shabby" in shabby chic. He made millions of dollars. I barely scraped by. Republican and Democrat. Staunch Catholic and apostate. We became Richie and Marcia. While he anglicized his last name to Simms, I ethnicized mine, taking the feminine form of our family name so I'd be more like my foremothers in Poland.

What we had in common was our household, our shared parents, and bearing witness to their incendiary relationship. What we had in common was being sent to the neighborhood tavern to bring our father home. What we had in common was a desire to keep our mother alive and out of harm. What we had in common was loving our grandparents and the peace it gave us when we stayed with them. What we had in common was fear.

My younger self was often a drag on my older brother. I hung around when he was with his boy pals, and I was a pest when he entertained his early dates. In response, he tormented me. He teased mercilessly. He flicked his finger and inflicted pain. He pinched. In frustration, I would try to hit him but always failed. Being two feet taller than I was, he could easily put a hand on my head, so that my weak punches could not reach his body. I felt powerless. When we watched our father strike our mother, we both felt powerless. We avidly watched boxing on TV.

One time, Dad hit Mom hard when she was cooking. In an uncharacteristic move, she grabbed the long-tined carving fork from the stove top and struck out at our father, grazing his face near his temple. What we kids had in common was hearing the story they made up to tell people about how he had scratched his head on a picture-hanging nail. When Richie turned 16, he boldly entered the middle of one of our parents' fights. By then, he was a head taller than his dad. But our father was a strong man who worked physically 10 hours a day. Richie threw out a punch. Dad flicked him away with the back of his hand.

What we had in common was that we couldn't protect our mother. What we had in common was shame.

A MADE MAN

My Uncle Stash "knew some guys." One time he asked me what size bathing suit I wore. Some size 12s had "fallen off the truck." Living in Chicago in the '50s, we grew up familiar with the Mafia. We would take family drives to look at their sprawling homes. The hospital where my Aunt Helene worked as a switchboard operator maintained a suite of rooms reserved especially for the big bosses "when the heat was on." Spontaneous attacks of appendicitis were not uncommon. They ordered room service and Helene joked with them on the phone. She knew their nicknames, their wives, their children.

Stash's connection had something to do with jukeboxes. I liked jukeboxes. I liked putting quarters in the slots and hearing my favorite tunes on demand. Fun, brightly-colored jukeboxes didn't fit in with what I knew about the Mafia from the movies. From the cinematic portrayals, I pictured burly Italian guys in fedoras bursting into spaghetti restaurants, demanding payoffs. Or street toughs in an alley bending back some other guys' fingers, insisting they better pay up "or else." My uncle was Polish and skinny. Everyone in the family called him "Junior." He looked more like a bike messenger than a bruiser. He told jokes. He took his nieces and nephews sledding in the snow. Still, people said he had "connections."

At a family party when I was 12, I overheard a conversation between my hero, the beloved Father Mitch, and my youngest and funnest uncle, Stash. They chatted amicably and then the priest stepped a little closer. He asked Stash if he might be able to land him some goods, "Y'know, prizes for the bingo games at the church." Stash, of course, said, "Anything for you, Father." I'm sure they went on to details, but I stopped listening. My two heroes had just crashed. The perfect man and the perfect uncle fell off their pedestals.

THE R.W. SIMMS BUILDING

My brother Rich in Phoenix with his two daughters.

My brother named a building after himself. The R.W. SIMMS building. Giant letters atop a downtown Phoenix tower broadcast his success loud and clear. The R.W. stood for Richard Walter, that much was familiar. Simms, on the other hand, was the name Rich had adopted when he fled the family to get married at age 20. He had had enough of our difficult family and troublesome ethnic background. He flew into the arms of a pretty Italian-American woman who was said to be an heiress. Her ancestors, the Ponterelli family, had installed the entire sewage system of Chicago. But, due to her parents' divorce, Annette had not grown up in the lap of luxury. She was sweet and kind and madly in love with my brother.

Annette's mother and her family hosted a series of bridal showers and engagement parties in Lincoln Park homes and downtown high-rise apartments. The wedding reception was in a posh downtown Chicago hotel where a flock of bridesmaids—myself included—wore chic plum-colored satin and velvet dresses. Anxiety-stricken about tripping or saying the wrong thing, I ended up sprouting a nasty cold sore above my lip that seemed as big as a dinner plate to my teenaged eyes. If you squint, you can spot it in the photos.

The morning of the wedding, my mother painted her nails to coordinate with the wedding colors. Since her fingertips were still sticky, she asked my Aunt Gerry to write out her generous check to the newlyweds. Mom intended to sign it later, just before putting it in the envelope. In the flurry of donning coats and tooting cars, she forgot to sign the check. For decades, she blamed herself for this neglect. Feeling abandoned by her only son, she said it was the reason behind the decades-long family cutoff. Having had many urges to distance myself from my own childhood, I had other theories.

In a letter I wrote to my friend Howard Bahr shortly after attending my father's funeral, I recounted an explosion between our mom, Rich, and Annette:

> My brother is six-foot-four and weight 235 pounds. His wife looks the same as I remembered, and my 2 nieces look like me. They felt my mother had hurt them deeply 8 years ago and never got over it. They have a story of pain to match every one my mother has. Sometimes the same incident was cited to me. All misunderstandings. How can people not see each other for six years like that without ever

talking about what's bothering them. Dates, hours, minutes were cited as to when my mother said this, or my brother said that. I couldn't believe it. My brother didn't want to give my mother any of the insurance money. She didn't ask. She can have mine. She doesn't want it.

Flash forward a couple of decades. Rich and I hadn't seen each other in years. He had never met my new family, so while we were visiting my first husband Bill's brother in Tucson, I had an urge to try to find my brother. I grew bold with the telephone. Why not give it a shot? To my surprise, Rich welcomed the visit. He had built a printing empire, made a million dollars, named a building after himself. With a twinge of sibling meanness, I murmured under my defensive and ethnically proud breath, "He named an f-ing building after himself! And it's not his real name."

Rich treated us to lunch at his country club, an oasis in the desert, thousands of sprinklers keeping the grass green and the birds-of-paradise in bloom. He proudly announced how he had paid $50,000 to join. For dinner, he treated us to a meal at a steakhouse where he knew the owner. Rich, I would learn, always knew the owner. He ordered huge platters of meat for each of us. Our four-year-old Inge plunged into the giant porterhouse like a Dickens character set free. Her pinky-ring-wearing uncle was delighted.

Decades passed with few phone calls. I invited him to my second wedding. I was divorced and was marrying a second academic. By this time, Rich was divorced and had gone through a bankruptcy. But Rich knew he was going to get a break any day now. He told me he was sure of it. On a short drive, he told me how miserable our childhood had been. He remembered overdone eggs and underdone pork. I remembered my mother as an excellent cook. I remembered Sunday drives to eat at a lovely country inn. He remembered our parents drinking too much and slurring their speech. Is memory reliable at all (she wrote while writing a book devoted to memory)? We both remembered how the teenaged Rich had taken a swing at our dad in an attempt to keep our father's fist from connecting with our mother's jaw.

Six months after my second wedding, I was diagnosed with breast cancer. My brother surprised me by calling every Tuesday evening after he went to church to pray for me. He had kept his religion but changed his name; I had lost my religion but kept my name. He teased me about keeping my "moniker," but was diligent and devoted about his prayers for my recovery.

Rich made a trip to the Midwest to visit the locations of his youth. The bakery. His high school. Our beloved grandfather's farm. I went with him to Atchison, Kansas to visit the college he attended for one year. Meantime, St. Benedict's College had changed its name to the Benedictine College and become co-ed, but many of the old buildings remained. On the way back, Rich asked for a loan. A few thousand till things got better. He paid me back faithfully in installments.

REJECTION

My kindergarten teacher rejected one of my earliest creations. Sister Mary Crescentine was my first teacher and my first love. I adored her. I wanted to be in her classroom forever. I wanted her to take me home with her.

One day, Sister Crescentine brought out finger paints. Our beloved teacher was going to allow us to dirty our hands in the name of art. She handed out a piece of paper to each of us along with a single color of fingerpaint. We were going to paint! With our fingers! We wore little aprons to protect our school uniforms. I was excited to see the colors as they were distributed. Dennis got green. Bonita got red. They set about covering their pages with flowers and blades of grass. Sister Mary Crescentine gave me a little pot of something that looked brown. Not yellow, not blue. Brown. The color of dirt and poop. I worried over what to do with this dull, lifeless color. I dawdled. I squished paint with my fingers, enjoying the sensation, despite my inability to come up with a concrete picture.

Suddenly, an idea occurred to me. I knew what I wanted to do. I made a series of rectangles within rectangles within rectangles, like picture frames inside of other picture frames. Sister Crescentine asked each of us what we had created. When it came to my turn, I stood up and answered, "A picture inside a picture inside a picture inside a picture." All the other children's pictures went up on display. Not mine. I was never allowed to fingerpaint again. Any aspirations I might have had to be a visual artist ended.

A few decades later, when I was living in Bloomington, Indiana, I belonged to a state writers' organization that held an annual meeting in Indianapolis. They invited me to give a talk and be on a panel. On the wall situated behind the registration desk was a large corkboard covered with the rejection notices that members had received in the last year. Hundreds of little anonymous Xeroxed slips of paper tacked up alongside long letters filled with regretful prose. I loved this public display of the multitude of rejections that writers experience with great frequency. I wanted all writers' conferences to follow suit, though I never saw this elsewhere. It let us know that we were not alone in our rejected status. It was part of the life of a writer, an artist.

I rarely receive a notice of rejection anymore. It's not that I don't get rejected. It's that these days, they often don't tell you. Silence means *no*. You can wait six months. You can wait a year. You can ask yourself if they are still reading, if you've been moved up to a short list. Or maybe your brilliant piece of prose was lost in the mail, in the cloud, in the void. Eventually, a year or two later, you have to come to terms with the fact that you've been turned down. Without so much as a text.

FAME & SHAME

Mom and me on her visit to New York for
my graduation and engagement.

My friend Xenia suggested we meet at the Russian Tea Room on 57th Street. I had dined at her family's home many times and she wanted to meet my mother, who was visiting New York for my graduation. I loved the Tea Room, with its polished samovars and attentive waiters, its refined atmosphere and elegant table settings. My mother would love it too. I just knew it. We planned to meet outside.

The day was cool and windy. My mom was wearing a shapeless blue cloth raincoat and, on her head, a black babushka with neon red roses printed around the edges. What? I wondered where her own self had disappeared. What had happened to the woman who had held her head up high in designer dresses, leather coats, and high heels while her world fell apart? What happened to the sleek, polished businesswoman who looked like Elizabeth Taylor? Instead, she resembled the immigrant housewives of my childhood. In my eyes, she now looked, in the admittedly derisive language of my old neighborhood, like she had "just gotten off the boat." I noticed things I had never seen before: a bit of a hooked nose, the olive tone of her skin. The dreadful wool babushka. I was ashamed. And next, I was ashamed of being ashamed.

When I was little, we kids had a gesture for shaming. We would point the index finger of our left hand out toward the miscreant, and, with the index finger of our right hand we'd swipe the left finger in the direction of the person we wanted to shame. "Shame on you!" we'd cry. "Shame on you."

In this case, shame on me.

I recalled the time when I was rummaging through my mother's dresser drawers, looking for something for playing dress-up. Hidden among her lacy things was a newspaper article about the federal forgery case against my father. It was years later, but I still felt embarrassed and humiliated. The neighbors, the mothers of my friends, knew. My father was famous. My father was infamous. My father was someone I felt ashamed of.

When articles or reviews come out about me or my work, I often have someone else eyeball them before I myself can read what they say. Maybe I fear that there will be a photo of me in handcuffs. Perhaps I dread the public's finding out about my own misdeeds. When accepting prizes, I never want to go to the podium and proudly accept them. I have sometimes wished that others would win so that people would not turn to look at me. Just in case something shameful is revealed.

Fame. Shame.
And...
Sorry, Mom.

MY OWN PERSONAL DONALD

Written in response to the ME, TOO movement & posted on Facebook

He was a man in his fifties, president of the publishing company where I worked. I was 19, taking some time off college after recuperating from a serious illness. Mr. Cloud called me into his office. I was excited, thinking I was going to be congratulated for having done something meritorious. I had already received a promotion and my editor had recently written a letter supporting my application to Barnard College, saying I was a "pioneer in the publishing field." Perhaps more kudos were coming my way. Mr. Cloud closed his office door and waved me closer to where he was standing at his desk. I eagerly walked toward him. He took my hand and placed it on the fly of his pants. He said, "This is what you do to me," indicating his erection. He held my hand there while he told me about the private yacht he had and how he'd like me to join him there. I pulled my hand away and walked out of the room.

He was not the first to transgress. An elderly relative I was supposed to tuck in for a nap had put his hand up my skirt and into my underwear. A priest had forced an open-mouthed, tongued kiss on me at my parents' home. A delivery man had pushed me to the ground and groped my developing breasts.

And he was not the last. At an anti-Vietnam war rally, a National Guardsman threw me to the ground and called me a "peace creep whore." My first day in New York to attend Barnard, a man tackled me in the park area at the Cloisters and attempted to rape me. I fought him off with my fists and knees, yelling and realizing in that moment that I might actually be capable of killing someone in order to defend myself. Later, a man I had had a relationship with and then jilted came back and did succeed in raping me. I knew him so I didn't expect it. The Artistic Director of a theatre brutally criticized a play I had written over coffee and then said, "Now we go to your motel room."

No. No. No. This can't go on.

When I was young, I never heard of reporting such transgressions. I was told about "funny uncles" and "locker-room talk" and "boys will be boys." I was left feeling brutalized and humiliated. I felt diminished and less likely to be taken seriously for my work or my worth. I told my friends, but I knew of no one to report to.

I am proud of the women who are speaking out in the wake of Donald Trump's sexual braggadocio. I remember every detail about my own personal Donald and his office on that day of my first real job when I thought I had done good work only to be reduced to somewhere to insert a penis. I remember his hairstyle and what he wore and the exact layout of his office. And I remember the exact words that he said, that this is what I did to him. What I did to him? I to him? When I hear the details of these women's stories, I believe they are remembering too. The face, the room, what was said that was supposed to make it our fault. Some things you never forget.

NOTE: A man I had dated in my twenties responded to this post, blaming me, saying that I had always tantalized men.

Saying Goodbye

REVISTING THE OLD NEIGHBORHOOD

My husband Tom wanted us to visit my old neighborhood while we were in Chicago. He had asked me to go on several previous visits to Chicago and I had always refused. But this time I caved.

I was prepared for everything to look smaller than I remembered. Friends had warned me about the "You can never go home again" phenomenon. But I didn't expect to feel such a sense of loss. I felt like a foreigner, an invader. Yes, I recognized the sidewalks where I played hopscotch and jumped rope as a child. And, there were the monkey bars where I used to hang upside down in the neighbor's yard. There was the alley where horse-drawn wagons would pass, selling produce or collecting rags for recycling into paper. I could almost hear the street cries in my head, "Peaches! Ripe peaches! Come and get your apricots!" "Rag-man. Ragman." Have I really lived long enough for there to have been peddlers with horse-drawn carts buying and selling in my neighborhood? Yes, and although it was a living memory for me, it seemed as if it belonged to some other person's life. It couldn't possibly have been in my own lifetime. And it all looked so different now. Painted with a different palette.

We stood outside the old address of 2501 N. Lotus Avenue. The fake redbrick tarpaper was gone and replaced with another inexpensive, less interesting, gray covering. The Casey's Pastry Shop neon sign was gone. I expected that yet mourned its absence anyway.

Tom wanted to go inside. Reluctantly, I walked into the bakery. Except it was no longer a bakery. Yes, they sold bread, but they also sold crackers and milk, canned soup, and greeting cards. It was a corner store. My family's bakery had disappeared. Someone had stolen my childhood. Okay, the bones of the building were still there, and they still baked bread, but everything about the place was different, wrong.

We walked around the tiny aisles, everything unfamiliar, strange. Yet memories came crashing in anyway: How grown up I had felt at age six to stand on top of a chair in order to reach the grand old register and enter a sale all by myself. The numbering system, the glass display cases, the bolt of string hanging from the ceiling. Gone but present.

The woman behind the counter started fidgeting. We were lingering too long for comfort. She asked, in a Polish accent, if we wanted anything. I shook my head, "No," but Tom revealed that I had grown up in the bakery, that my parents used to own it, decades ago. She understood this journey and invited us to walk around behind the store, to revisit the home of my childhood.

We did. Tom had never seen any of it, so it seemed perfectly normal to him. I was shocked at the closed-in gloom of it all. The storeroom where my brother and I used to fashion aprons into capes and lift aluminum "chalices" to play Mass had absolutely no windows. Nor did my first bedroom. Where was the silly joy of the kitchen where my mother's parakeet Skippy would ride on the head of her dog, Cinders.

So much of the building being windowless and dark made me realize that I had spent a great deal of my childhood not here at all, but out on the sidewalk, in the alley and in the yards of neighbors, out in the sun and light. In the summers, I had been sent to stay with grandparents or aunts and uncles where, again, I was out of doors. That's what childhood was to me. Playing outside—statue maker, crack the whip—and then coming inside only to eat, to listen to my parents argue, fight, hit.

I was awakened from my memory by our tour guide, the new owner. She took us back to the shop, where the giant wood-topped tables were, where the deep brick oven was, where my father and his crew of bakers had created thousands of loaves of bread. I recalled how my father guarded his recipes for rye and pumpernickel bread closely. "I begged him to tell me," my mother would say. He died with his secrets.

As I stood silently, blankly staring at a giant mixer, almost drooling over the memory of my father's bread, I heard myself being addressed, as if our host could read my mind. "Here. Here. Take this. From us." And she handed me a loaf of warm, dark bread. Made in this bakery. Tom nodded his head toward the doorway. A signal. We may have overstayed our welcome. The woman needed to get back to her cash register, to greeting customers, making sales. She had been kind to let us walk through the dark, gloomy house. She had been kind to give us a loaf of pumpernickel bread. I put on a sunny smile, but a quiet darkness was invading my interior. I was not ready to leave my memories yet. Memories that had become the stuff of much of my work.

Mom, Rich, and me in front of the house part of the bakery building on his First Communion Day.

VISITING BUSIA

My grandmother moved into a senior apartment building. Since her early widowhood, she had been moving around among the homes of her six children. When an apartment building for age 50+ residents opened in our suburb of Niles, everyone in the family was overjoyed. Especially my beloved Busia. Where other people saw a blandly modernist apartment building surrounded by dirt, she saw an opportunity to surround a large building with flowers. She especially loved planting pansies because, not only did they bloom twice a year, but they looked like little smiling faces looking up at her.

When I came home for vacation, I visited her. She'd make a yummy tomato soup and we'd chat. When I asked her what the biggest problem being her age was, she answered, "Sex. The men think they can do it and they can't!" Apparently, there were a lot of flirtations in the senior housing project. Men were at a premium since they tended to die younger. She wasn't interested in anyone, she said blushingly. She had a small living room, kitchen, and a little bedroom all to herself. Busia loved it there. She sat knitting bandages ("for the soldiers," she told me, as if we were in WWII) or crocheting caps and scarves for me and the other grandchildren.

When I returned to New York, she started sending me her Social Security check of $33 per month. It would be worth at least ten times that now, I'm sure. It was a great help to me, but I worried about her. When she was no longer able to take care of herself, she moved in with my mother and her new husband, at 7000 Jonquil Terrace, where my uncle Stash and his younger son had also taken refuge after a divorce.

When I was 24, I spent half my time on a friend's farm in the Berkshires. One night, my mom called on my friend's phone. As soon as I heard her voice, I screamed, "Nooooo!" I knew it meant that my Busia had died. My mother said she had taken her to the hospital, but they couldn't save her. Busia tried to speak, to say her final words of wisdom or joy or comfort or regret, but they had put a metal device in her mouth, and she could not. They had put so many tubes in her arms that she could not move her arms about, she could not gesture, could not speak with her hands. She had struggled against the machinery, trying to say her last words, but the great storyteller of my life could not speak. My grandmother, who had meant so much to me as a child, was gone.

For weeks afterward, I kept feeling that I wanted to talk with Busia, to tell her about how the farm where I was staying brought back memories of her farm. I wanted to catch her up on my life, to tell her that I was in love, that I was writing a play, riding horses, picking raspberries, and making jam. I felt that my own mouth was stuffed with cotton. I felt silenced by her death. I felt this way for years until a friend told me that I could still talk to her. Not through some medium or Ouija board, but just ordinary chat. And so, I began to talk to her when I was alone and also through my work, my words on the page. She had been my model of a storyteller, after all, and I loved sharing what I was doing with her, with the version of her that lives on in memory.

ON THE SKIDS

My father died a homeless man. Pneumonia. Cirrhosis of the liver. He was 54.

People told me he'd been spiraling downhill since the divorce. After we'd moved to the suburbs to save my parent's marriage. After selling the business to lower the stress and save the marriage. After my mother's getting pregnant to save the marriage. After she lost the baby. After they lost the marriage.

My father had visiting rights to see me on Sunday afternoons. He would come around on those Sundays and ask me how I was doing, inquire about my cousin Wally, my Aunt Helene. Every Sunday afternoon, I watched and waited for these glimpses of my father. Before the divorce, I had been so frightened of him, the 13-year-old me had barricaded him out of the house. But now that he was out, I waited anxiously for his visits. I was desperately trying to understand. He was my father. He was part of the clay out of which I was made. Was I scarred by his abuse of my mother? Was I going to be like him? Was there some good in him that could be salvaged?

He visited dutifully for months. At Christmastime, he brought me a gift in a small velvet box. A golden wristwatch. A Bulova. A watch for a grown-up. I wore it proudly. I stroked it at school, distracted from Church History by wondering what else he might bring me. Maybe he had learned his lesson and was going to be a better dad. I looked forward to his next visit.

He never came back.

When I was 18, Dad called me and asked me to come visit him at a TB sanitorium. My mother drove me there. My father gave me a leather wallet he had made in a crafts class on the campus of the hospital. I still have that wallet, unused in my dresser. I do not know why I keep it or why I have his watch chain or why I keep waiting for answers.

After giving me the wallet, he asked me for a couple thousand dollars. I was a student and had nothing to give him. By then, I was brimming with anger toward him for his abandonment. Should I have emptied my change purse of coins and dollar bills? Would that have made a difference?

When I was a student at Barnard, and for several years thereafter, I worked at the Bureau of Applied Research at Columbia University on the Homelessness Project, a sociological study based on life-history interviews of homeless people. We staff members called it the Bowery Project. While I was compiling an annotated bibliography and interviewing homeless people, my father was, unknown to me, living on Skid Row in Chicago.

Recently, Howard Bahr, who had been the Project Director for the Homelessness Project, not knowing that I was writing this book, mailed me a few letters that I had sent him during that time. One of them reads, in part:

Then came the news.

My father was dying. I had never made the connection between the Bowery study and my father until then. He was found unconscious and perhaps beaten up in a ratty old hotel. He was taken to Cook County Hospital with pneumonia caused by anemia caused by cirrhosis.

It was a wait for death.

I paced the floor for three days with a sense of fear. Then I took a plane to Chicago so that maybe the fear would go away and with the excuse that I would make my mother feel better. My brother was taking care of everything. My brother who refused to see my mother for the last six years and who hadn't seen my father in ten. My brother, Richard Simms. My father improved and got worse. We were told he would die any minute, then his condition was improved.

I was warned not to see him but went anyway. He looked 70 and yellow and had arms the width of two fingers. All stuffed with tubes and machinery and with a mouth full of blood, he looked at me with a very soft blue-gray eye. He died that night.

The wake with people saying that if it wasn't for my mother, that would never have happened to him. That he loved her until the day he died. That she should have taken him back. No mention of the tears and bottles drunk or horses raced or beatings given or of the nights, days, weeks of waiting for him to come back in those "happy, early days." She was noble to be there after ten years of divorcedness. I admired her.

THE SINS OF THE FATHER

My father left me three thousand dollars in insurance money. My brother suggested that I buy myself a VW bug. Instead, I travelled to South America to visit college friends who worked for the State Department. After three months of travelling by horseback through Chile and experiencing a 7.6 earthquake in Peru, I had barely landed in New York when I took off again. This time to Europe with two of my New York friends. From Luxembourg, we traveled around Central Europe. I parted paths with them in Poland, where I stayed on as long as I could. I ventured on to the Czech Republic, Austria, and Italy. When it was time, I returned to Luxembourg to take a plane back home. I had almost no money.

Flat broke, I went to the American Embassy, and they surprised me by calling my mother, asking her to telegraph cash so that I could buy my plane ticket home. I waited day after day for the money to come. In spite of encroaching winter, I stayed in unheated hotels. I begged coins off tourists who were about to leave the country. I ate day-old bread that had been dumped behind a bakery. I waited. Unfortunately, my mother had sent the money to Luxembourg, Germany, not the country of Luxembourg. More days passed. Winter was upon us. The hotelier took pity and moved me to a heated room.

Eventually, the money came and I was able to board a plane to New York City, but I needed to go home, to Chicago, to my mother. I was feeling sad, lonely, sick. I hitchhiked with someone I met on the plane. We were lucky most of the time, but the hitchhiking laws in Ohio were strict and the snow heavy. We slept in sleeping bags on the interstate meridian as the snow accumulated.

By the time I reached Chicago, I had trouble standing. When I called my mother to ask her to pick me up, the little holes in the acoustical tile surrounding the public telephone booth seemed to shake and spin.

The doctor said I had completely exhausted my health and now had the heart of a 50-year-old businessman. My father had been 54 when he died. My liver, he said, already damaged from an earlier bout of hepatitis, was also in danger. My father had died of cirrhosis of the liver. My mother's care and soup helped bring me back to life.

A few years later, my mother asked me to clear out some boxes in the basement. I went through old report cards and glossy photos of me dancing in Hawaiian skirts. Among the memorabilia was an old address book. I recalled that it had gone missing, and I assumed I had lost it on the trip home from that first trip to Europe. I was turning the pages, seeing the names of college and New York friends, reminiscing, when five 20-dollar bills dropped out onto the basement floor. I recalled some advice my mother had given me before I took that trip: hide cash in various places: put it in your underwear, the pockets of your suitcase, your address book. I had followed her advice but then, after months of travel, forgot where I had hidden the money. I had stopped looking in my address book when I was panhandling for survival. I had stopped sending postcards.

Some might say my travel had something to do with my grief. Some might say I was replicating, in some fashion, my father's homelessness by wandering from place to place. And maybe they'd be right. Leaving everything behind, running my body into the ground, living in squalor and on the kindness of strangers. Like him, I'd become a bum. Yet all the while, I had this little cache.

Now I wonder, was it random that I worked on the Homelessness Project? That I wandered from place to place like my father? That I have written four adaptations of Homer's *Odyssey?* With every relationship I've had, I've worried about being abandoned. For years, I asked my husband Tom if he was going to leave me. "I'm not going anywhere," he always reassures me. I have seen therapists. I have written about my father several times in plays. Writing has been the best therapy.

This book has been a balm.

A EULOGY FOR MOM

My mother died in 2005. Cleaning out a desk drawer recently, I came across the reading I gave at her funeral. I am not even sure I would grace it with the word "eulogy." It was short and I tried for my mother's humanity rather than a praise poem. Here is what I said:

Marcia's eulogy for her mom 11/8/05

I've known my mom all my life, so when the newspaper obituary was written—wife, mother, grandmother, great-grandmother—I thought there were a few things left out about my mom, who, over the years was also:

-An astute businesswoman
-A balancer of books
-A generous giver
-A Mother's Club president
-A Raindrop
-A Sweet Adeline
-An accomplished player of Chopin
-An alluring flirt
-A chocoholic

She drank martinis with nuns,
> *Went to masquerade parties in harem pants,*
> *Danced the can-can to raise money for the Church.*
She wore gloves to Marshall Fields.

She hated war, injustice, and itchy sheets.
She loved dogs, lobster tail, things purple, God.
She sang opera while patting out pizza dough.
She made the best soup.
She cried too easily,
> *Laughed too readily,*
> *For some people's taste.*
It was the Polish in her.
She had trouble walking,
> *She danced like a feather.*
She was no longer able to speak,
> *She sang with her whole soul.*
She suffered much pain,
> *Endured much loneliness,*
> *Laughed deeply,*
> *Loved passionately.*
She was Kazia, Corky, Casmira, Casey, Darling, Mommy, Honey, Busia, Dear One, Kochana, Mom.
She once explained to me that we all have to die to make room on this earth for those to come.
We'll miss her.

FAREWELL TO RICHARD

My brother reappeared just in time. When he was diagnosed with late-stage colon cancer, Tom and I made a trip to Phoenix. I froze a gigantic pot of chicken soup so it would pass through airport security. While we sat watching TV in the evenings, his phone rang insistently with calls from creditors. He didn't answer the calls. He went into his second bankruptcy.

Rich called again when he had two weeks to live. Before we entered the hospice room, his ex-wife warned me that he didn't look like himself. Instead of the robust man he had been, he was skeletal yet swollen. I wasn't sure how to be helpful. At his bedside, I held his hand and told him stories of our childhood. Especially of our time together on our grandparents' farm. I sang songs. The nurse took his vitals and said she was truly amazed. All of his vital signs had improved dramatically.

His daughters were at his bedside. His sons-in-laws and grandchildren came to say goodbye. We waited around his bed in vigil mode. After rehearsing the words a few dozen times, I held his hand and told him it was all right if he left. While we waited, my Tom put up a slideshow of the photos of our new grandson. Through the slides, we all watched an infant discovering his new world for the first time. Rich departed silently with these images of newborn life playing before him.

SOOOOOOO BIG!!!!!

My first memory is of baby me standing up, albeit unsteadily, in our claw-footed bathtub. In this memory, I am wet from head-to-toe, having recently been bathed by my mommy. I am grinning, because I know what is coming. My mommy, her arms surrounding me so I don't fall on the soapy tub, says, "How big is Marcia?" I reach my hands above my head as high as I can and she says, "So big!" She says it again and again, "Soooo big!" and I try to say the words. I utter something like, "Ooooo ig!" and I say it loudly with joy and enthusiasm. My mommy wraps me up in a big clean towel and scoops me up from the tub into her arms. I am giggling and snuggling and in love with the notion that I have grown so big and, even better, I can say words! What power! For the next year or so, I cling to this gesture, sometimes executed one-handedly, sometimes two-handed, enjoying my newfound stature and ability to stand up and speak up.

APPENDIX:
EXCERPTS FROM CREATIVE WORK

The saints and sinners whose stories I've touched on in this book shaped my writing and my life. In this section are short excerpts from my creative work, tidbits from my plays and fiction that were inspired by real-life experiences alluded to in this memoir.

FLORIDA

When writing my play Florida, *I relied heavily on recollections of my childhood, including my mother's Floridian fantasies. In this scene, Sophie comforts her nightmare-prone daughter Cindy with visions of Florida.*

SOPHIE
[pauses, comforts CINDY]
Florida. Even name sounds like flowers. Flowers everywhere. On trees and bushes, climbing up vines. You know the red flowers we have on altar at Christmas?

CINDY
Point-settas.

SOPHIE
Yes, these are huge in Florida, as big as your head and growing on trees, even in winter.

CINDY
And birds. I want to hear about the birds.

SOPHIE

There are pink birds--pink!!! With so long legs they look like they are walking on stilts. And parrots. There is this place, Parrot Jungle, where there are hundreds of parrots. Green and blue and purple. They will sit on your arms and your head even and pull the bobby pins right out of your hair.

CINDY

And fruit.

SOPHIE

Oranges and grapefruits and peaches growing right in people's yards. And so sweet. I think it is what-you-call—where Adam and Eve were—

CINDY

The Garden of Eden.

SOPHIE

Yes, I think it is Garden of Eden, this Florida.

———————

In this next and last excerpt from Florida, *Bruno, a baker who is accused of breaking into the family safe and forging bonds, argues with his wife, Sophie. In order to write the character modeled on my father, I had to do something akin to getting into his skin. I had to know, understand, and inhabit him. Since I had spent decades of my life ferociously angry with him, this was a challenge.*

———————

BRUNO

Shhh! Okay, quiet, everything is going to be all right.

SOPHIE

Just tell me what did you do with this money? What? Tell me!!

BRUNO

Listen to me, please. Okay? Shhh. I had dream for us. I was buying ten freezers and ten trucks. Bread and cakes going to every part of city. Everyone eating **my** bread. Yes, I went to the track, just needing little more to make true. Then I would make big money. Send children to Harvard. Just listen to me, Sophie. I felt so lucky, like touched by the God. It was perfect blue day. My blood, it was racing with these horses. I felt ALIVE!! ALIVE, you hear? And I was winning. Doubling money. I was almost to bursting with excitement. BURSTING! And then, something, it goes bad. Bad!! Like upside down.

[pause]

I couldn't bear to tell you!

SOPHIE

Future for children, all gone?!

THE BONES OF BUTTERFLIES

When I heard about millions of Monarch butterflies dying in a freeze in Mexico, I immediately imagined my homeless father, freezing on a street corner. I drafted a play called The Bones of Butterflies *in which a butterfly scientist searches for her missing father. Honoring my dad's artistry in cake decoration, I made the character parallel to my father: a concert guitarist. At the end of the play, freezing butterflies fall from the trees as we hear the tale of the father's decline.*

DIEGO

When the great Malinowski played, even the trees listened. He flew from city to city to perform. When the guitarist grew too old to play in the great concert halls, he made music outside on the plaza, the Zocalo. He lived in a small hotel. During the day, people saw him walking, enjoying the sunlight.

He was familiar. People put coins in his guitar case.

The day came when he could no longer afford the small hotel. He was the old man on the corner. Women brought him tortillas. Nuns covered his head.

One day, a wind blew. A hard rain started to fall. The rain froze.
It coated the trees, like glass.

I am so sorry to tell you.

Your father was found.

I am sorry to tell you.

Your father was found.

DEAR JOHN

I wrote Dear John *in epistolary form. I thought the letter-writing conveyed the idea of emotional closeness and physical distance, as in my relationship to Bob DeChristopher. Below is the first letter of the play. Interesting that in the play, I flipped reality and made the woman the one to leave the relationship. If only.*

EMILY

Dear John,

Go to hell. This is the end. I'm on a plane to South America right now, running away. You'll think that I'm a rotten awful coward of a woman, of course. I believe I'm being quite reasonable.

Anyway, thank you for some of the deepest, most meaningful moments of my life. The most profound joy and anguish I ever hope to experience I owe to you. There's no one like you, you beautiful shit.

Don't try to find me. You won't. South America is a very big place.

Yours truly,
Emily

P.S. Sincere apologies for any inconvenience I may have caused. I'll never forget you. Good-bye forever.

Love,
Em

VISIONS OF RIGHT

Visiting Auschwitz was a powerful experience, which became even more potent when I saw my own name on a label identifying an inmate's photograph. When writing my play Visions of Right, *responding to the anti-gay ministry of the Westboro Baptist Church, I called on that experience.*

OZ

There's no way to convey to you. . . We walk in . . .

CHRISTINA

And see a mountain of suitcases—different sizes, colors, marked with the names of people. And their addresses, the places they hoped to return to. And I think, *Poor Jews.* And there's shoes piled up taller than me. Wooden and leather, men's, women's, children's. Real shoes from real people. You can smell them. Behind a window, hundreds of eyeglasses of every shape. *Poor Jews.*

OZ

We see the ovens, unspeakable "scientific experiments." I can't bear it anymore, so I go off.

CHRISTINA

We get separated somehow. I search the halls, lost, alone, guiltily wandering. *Poor Jews, Poor Jews.* I am roaming corridors lined with hundreds, maybe thousands of photographs. Photographs of the victims—each one with shaved head, striped prison garb, a number, a name, and then, I see her. Just across from me. At eye level. Her photograph with **my name**. The Polish version of my name. Shorn hair. Striped shirt. My name. Krystyna Romanek.

[light up on]   REV. JONES
Fag Jew Sodomite Whore.

                    CHRISTINA
My people.

                    REV. NOAH
The chaff must burn!
I said the chaff must burn!

NOW LET ME FLY

I had the great honor of being commissioned to write a play for the national celebration of the 50th anniversary of the Brown v. Board *Supreme Court decision marking the end of legalized racial segregation. The first words I composed were for a monologue to represent the speech the teenage Barbara Johns gave before her school assembly. I based it on interviews with her fellow strikers and her own diary. Below is an excerpt from my play,* Now Let Me Fly.

BARBARA JOHNS

Every morning I get on a bus thrown away by the white high school on the hill. I sit on a torn seat and look out a broken window. And when my bus passes the shiny new bus that the white high schoolers have, I hide my face because I'm embarrassed in my raggedy bus. And when we get to R. R. Moton High, the bus driver gets off with us, because he's also our history teacher. He comes in the classroom and fires up the stove and I sit in my winter coat waiting for the room to get warm. You know the rooms, the ones in the "addition" as they call it. We call them "the tar paper shacks" because that's what they are, am I right? I'm embarrassed that I go to school in tar paper shacks and when it rains, I have to open an umbrella so the leaks from the roof won't make the ink run on my paper. And later in the day I have a hygiene class out in that broken-down bus and a biology class in a corner of the auditorium with one microscope for the whole school. I'm embarrassed that our water fountains are broken and our wash basins are broken and it seems our whole school is broken and crowded and poor. And I'm embarrassed. But my embarrassment is nothing compared to my hunger. I'm not talking about my hunger for food. No, I'm hungry for those shiny books they have up at Farmville High. I want the page of the Constitution that is torn out of my social studies book. I want a chance at that *Romeo and Juliet* I've heard about but they tell me I'm not fit to read. Our teachers say we can fly just as high as anyone else. That's what I want to do. Fly just as high. I said, fly. You know, I've been sitting in my embarrassment and my hunger for so long that I forgot about standing up. So, today, I'm going to ask you to stand with me. Before we fly, before we fly just as high as anyone else, we gotta walk just as proud as anyone else. And that's what we're going to do! We're gonna walk out of this school and over to the courthouse. Do you hear me? We're gonna walk with our heads high and go talk to the school board. Are you with me? We're gonna walk out in a strike, yes, I said strike, and we won't come back until we get a real school with a gymnasium and library and whole books. And we will get them. And it'll be grand. Are you with me? Are we gonna walk? Are we gonna fly?

WATCHING MEN DANCE

In the novel Watching Men Dance, *I called upon childhood memories of making beet horseradish for Polish Easter to write about my main character's visit to Chicago.*

Everything Dottie says is true: the crying and nipped fingertips and overwhelming nostril-antagonizing pungency. The little girls, in aprons tied under their armpits, first turn up their noses, then each try a bite of boiled beet. Xenia dutifully chews and swallows. Sequoia spits out the first taste but then grabs another, bigger piece. Dottie herself wears an apron that covers her from shoulders to mid-thigh in pockets and flowers. She jangles keys in one of the pockets as she instructs Julie how to add the vinegar and salt. When she's given a sample, Dottie screws up her face, "Strong! Bitter! Salty!" she exclaims. Dottie herself stirs in the deep purple grated beets, "Helps take the edge off, like a good joke in hard times." A pause and then Dottie, with a bit of a flourish, raises a full tablespoon of the mixture to her nose, then her mouth. Like a wine connoisseur she furrows her forehead, concentrates on the bouquet and the complexity of tastes. She nods her approval, "It's like life, right? You got the bitter and you got the sweet."

Acknowledgments

None of this without those who came before me.

None of this without the cousins and friends whose bread and words nourished the writer in me.

None of this without the storytellers, music makers, and dancers who continue to give our lives shape, purpose, and joy.

With gratitude for those who listened to the stories, read them on the page, and helped them mature with research, edits, comments, and encouraging words: Cecil Wooten, Louise Welch, Jeanne Rostaing, Wally Mika, Eric McHenry, Harriet Lerner, Steve Lerner, Emily Kofron, Martha Jacobs, Nan Hoffman, Jeffrey Ann Goudie, Caryn Mirriam-Goldberg, Andy Farkas, Tracey Cullen, Cathleen Bascom, Tim Bascom, and Tom Averill.

Thanks to Thea Rademacher, friend and editor supreme, for sharing my vision and embracing my dream.

Boundless appreciation to my Tom, who joined me on the trips to Poland and Chicago, who helped me with every research detail down to finding my grandmother's ship manifest, and always supporting my art, my work, always at my side.

All of this for those who come after me. For my daughter and grandson, Inge and Judah, these stories belong to you.

About the Author

Marcia Cebulska grew up in Chicago and has spent most of her career writing for the stage and screen. Her critically acclaimed plays have been produced at thousands of venues worldwide and her screenwriting aired on PBS. She has received the Jane Chambers International Award, the Dorothy Silver Award, several Master Artist Fellowships, and a National Endowment for the Arts commission. Marcia's guided journal SKYWRITING was released in 2019. Her novel WATCHING MEN DANCE was released in 2020. Marcia lives in Topeka, Kansas with her husband, historian Tom Prasch.

marciacebulska.com

Made in the USA
Middletown, DE
18 October 2023

41041072R00128